Instant Cordova Desktop Development

A Complete Practical Guide to Writing Cordova Apps

I0014761

To **Eva**, Laura, Bondi, Claudia and Chico.

"I'd rather die than lose my life"

To **Eva**: Write the $1mm app!

Instant Cordova Mobile Development

Copyright and Trademark Information

© 2017 Madvox LLC - All Rights Reserved
http://www.madvox.com

This book is provided for personal use and for informational purposes. We do not offer any warranties or representation, express or implied, with regards to the accuracy of the information presented here and we do not accept any liability for any loss or damage arising from the use of this book, any errors or omissions.

Madvox is a trademark of Madvox LLC. Other trademarks used in this book are the property of their respective owners and are used here for editorial purposes and to the benefit of the trademark owner. Terms used in this book are not intended to infringe on any trademark.

Introduction

About me

Before I write anything at all I want to share just a little bit about me so that you can get an idea of who I am and what I have done and what motivates me to write something like this. While I do not pretend to be an expert at any of the technologies discussed here, I am an expert at "everything" and I have a long history of writing mobile apps which I hope to share with you and that it is useful. I've published books and technical papers before so getting "published" is not my motivation. I want to offer this manuscript for free so there is no cost to you reading it or owning a copy of it.

I am a systems and software engineer with a great passion for Astronomy which is my real vocation. I worked for IBM Systems back in the 80's until I joined a private chemical company where I have been for the last 30 years mostly managing technical teams responsible for Research and Development, Engineering or Manufacturing Automation. I have experience also working with a great diversity of hardware from IT to manufacturing and of course, I've devoted great time to writing astronomy applications.

My background is primarily software engineering and software development. I started out in the mid 80's with the 8080 Processor and CP/M and some Unix variants - I bet some of you do not even know what this means. I moved on to work for IBM on DOS (version 1.x) and during that time I primarily wrote device drivers or assembly programs for the system. After I moved from IBM into the chemical manufacturing industry I did a variety of software development work (writing ledgers, invoicing, inventory systems, etc.) until I moved to manufacturing automation and also Research (scientific instrumentation and such) which is what I do best.

I went from being a hardware systems developer, to an applications developer, to a web developer, to a research developer and, during this time, I used many tools and languages. On the latter, I can tell you that I started out with ASM/MASM and moved to C, then to C++ (my primary language) and from there to Basic, Delphi, Java, JavaScript, C# and some other more specialized languages like Fortran, Ada, Lisp, Python, etc.

I have a number of applications in the stores that you are welcome to try to see my style. They are all free and ad-free for, as I mentioned before, I do this in the hope it is useful and not to make any money - that is not my driver. Your purchasing of the eBook itself is appreciated though if you wish to support me.

Assume you know nothing, even if you do

Important: If you want to skip everything and get directly to hands on app writing go **here** or **here** for the sample application code.

Note that I am not an expert in IOS so coverage of IOS is much shorter than other platforms. I am asking you to make this assumption that you know nothing for two reasons: first, I am targeting this book at people that are new or need to find their way from near zero to a running app in a store. So even if you already know how to do this, I hope you can find some bits of wisdom here that will help you in some way.

The second reason is - I want this to be a practical guide. Therefore, I will not be writing about why things are the way they are or, where Cordova came from or, its relationship to PhoneGap. I will not be teaching you how to program JavaScript or Typescript although I will be giving you resources to learn it easily if you wish. There is no point in me writing a JavaScript manual when there are so many good ones around. So, if you already know this then that is great and if you do not, I will help you find out how to learn these things.

Overall, what this section is trying to tell you is - do not look here for a transcendental in-depth manual on how to use certain tools and languages. This is more of an entry-level or intermediate dissertation on what exactly you need to know and do to get up and running with Cordova and other tools.

In many respects, this book also reflects my personal opinion on technology quite intensely. Where my personal opinion is stated, I will be sure to mark it in Italics or the color green, in a way that you understand that is what I think and it may not be mainstream or in line with other arguments.

Mobile Development

Why the focus on mobile development? Well, mobile development has been around for quite a while. I remember writing applications for PocketPC 2000 and also Midlets for regular Java phones at the beginning of this century (sounds like a long time ago!) You may remember machines like the Dell Axim v51 running Windows mobile or Windows CE; phones like the Motorola Razr V3 which allowed you to write applications as Java Midlets; the Zune, Palm, Motorola, Dell, Toshiba, Sega, so many others... I used to write mobile applications for those, including my games OddSun and OddMoon depicted below.

Mobile development was difficult then and this difficulty was not due to the technology. After all, writing a Java Midlet was not difficult.

The difficulty was the lack of unifying technologies - when you wrote something for a device it was very much set in stone, it was not portable, it was not very reusable and it was rigid and monolithic. There were no specific User Interface (UI) tools or application frameworks outside individual OEM's providing some starting points. Debugging was extremely difficult, there were few if any good emulators, you get the idea.

Today, mobile development has grown exponentially. Not only has the technology gotten to a point where reusability and quality are top priorities but also the devices themselves already come with everything you need to make your app work well, ranging from GPU's to UI frameworks and application frameworks. User Experience

(UX) and design guidelines are everywhere and while there is not a unified field here due to different requirements on different

devices, the field is not as fragmented as it once was and it continues to converge around some really good standards (for instance IOS' UI or Material from Google, etc.) This convergence is not simply centred on the UI and UX it applies also to development tools. It is increasingly frequent to find IDE's that support, well, pretty much everything from desktop to mobile to micro devices and Internet of Things (IoT).

This opens up one very good opportunity to truly write an app once and run it everywhere as Java said once. It is only now that this is possibly starting to come true. Do not get me wrong, we are not there yet by any means, as I will explain in more depth later, but we have taken some seriously giant steps forward and I love that.

Programming paradigms are continually shifting towards the better. Total decoupling of the UI and the UX from the code is absolutely necessary and, while we are not entirely there, we've been at it for a long time and we are almost there.

Speaking of paradigms, another thing (as an in-depth system developer) that has me extremely excited is the option to write no code in order to make an application. Once again, we are not quite there but I look forward to the day when I can design a complex app and not have to worry about meeting prerequisite structures required by different languages and IDE's. This also opens the door to designers that do not necessarily know or like coding, to writing great applications with minimal effort.

Mobile has also very much (de-facto perhaps) taken over the desktop for most day-to-day activities. The desktop is not dead - you still need it for a large variety of jobs (for instance, editing a complex spreadsheet on the phone is just not practical and having maximum field of view is very important). But for almost everything else, at least from a consumer perspective, mobile apps are where everything is at. I have written some typical desktop apps and ported them to mobile where it is easy and convenient to have certain information with you (for instance location of objects while you are at a telescope) and the result is simply far, far better.

Note also that with tools like Cordova, these apps will also run on your desktop with no code changes so in fact, you are achieving two things with just one shot (or code base). This is very important to developers as they can write it once and make simple adjustments for different platforms - no longer a need to write an app 3 times for 3 differing platforms. This is not true of native apps of course, but more on that later.

Mobile applications also benefit greatly from standardized application stores. I do not longer need to worry about how to package and distribute my app (a huge headache that could be 30 or 40 percent of my total effort). I just upload the app to a store, meeting certain requirements, and the entire business of packaging, distribution, deployment, tracking and anything else you can think of, is automatically taken care of.

It is because of things like this that I decided to focus on mobile for this work. However, I am not leaving the desktop nor the server aside so I will be giving you useful information on those as well. By the way, this also includes running your app on a browser like for instance Chrome, or even on specific services like Amazon Fire OS, FireFox OS and many others.

You may already be thinking about the implications and perhaps benefits of writing native apps for these platforms. Do not worry - I have a whole section below where we can discuss that at length.

What is Cordova

 I am originally from Spain so when I first read about Cordova, many years ago, I thought it was a misspelled version of the Spanish city of Córdoba, a city I have actually lived in for a number of years. But not at all - Cordova is a technology used to write "hybrid" applications that run on a variety of platforms and devices on the premise of one code base that runs everywhere.

More specifically, I can quote from the Apache Cordova site and say this:

"Apache Cordova is an open-source mobile development framework. It allows you to use standard web technologies - HTML5, CSS3, and JavaScript for cross-platform development. Applications execute within wrappers targeted to each platform, and rely on standards-compliant API bindings to access each device's capabilities such as sensors, data, network status, etc.

Use Apache Cordova if you are:

- *a mobile developer and want to extend an application across more than one platform, without having to re-implement it with each platform's language and tool set.*
- *a web developer and want to deploy a web app that's packaged for distribution in various app store portals.*
- *a mobile developer interested in mixing native application components with a WebView (special browser window) that can access device-level APIs, or if you want to develop a plugin interface between native and WebView components."*

I have a few enhancements of my own to make to the statements above:

1. Although Cordova is indeed designed for mobile development your applications will run on a variety of desktop platforms as well, including Windows (32/64) and Linux with some minor changes;

2. Although Apache's definition clearly single outs JavaScript there are other languages and certain variants of JavaScript that can be used with Cordova as well;

3. Cordova calls the final application "native" although it is not designed as a native application but it does behave as a native application, when all is said and done. More on this later since this requires some additional clarity;

4. The rest of Apache's statement is perfectly clear - this is very much like writing a web site and packaging it up as an application, with some notable differences discussed below.

So, there you have it - you are going to be using simple and familiar (if you are a web developer) technologies to build powerful applications that will run practically anywhere! I am not going very much in-depth on what Cordova is made of or what else it can do. This is deliberate on my part as I said before that I want to keep this work as a practical guide from 0-100% and thus, I see it unnecessary to go into any more depth. However, for those who want to see additional details on what Cordova is, please refer to the official site here:

https://cordova.apache.org/docs/en/latest/guide/overview/

On Cordova and Game Maker Studio

 Many years ago, my son (a designer) started working with Game Maker - this is before it was acquired by YoYo Games and turned into today's Game Maker Studio (which is even better!). At that time, probably around the year 2000 or so, I was writing games out of absolute enjoyment. I am not particularly good at writing games but I do try to do a good job (you can see some examples of my games in the stores - I will give you the links in the appendices).

At the time, I was writing my own engines for 2D platform games, shoot-them-up, jump-and-run, etc. Those are the types of games I liked to write and, with over 20 years of experience writing software, I was very comfortable writing my own engine or relying on things like DirectX 5 and 7 at the time.

Then my son came by and showed me a platformer he had written in two days using Game Maker. Not only was this platformer as good as anything I could write with tedious, meticulous and frankly complex C++ frameworks... it was actually better as it had a large variety of particles, parallax scrolling, automatic sprite animation, etc.

My first reaction when I saw game maker was - come on, that is not a professional tool. You may have done this impressive demo but surely you can't do surface blitting, pixel-perfect collisions, bone animations or anything of the sort. You need to write your own engine for total freedom.

It took me a long time to admit (and to change my programming stereotypes) that I was completely wrong. What Game Maker offered at the time was:

- An engine for 2D games that was already written and had every feature I could think of, including many I had not even written yet.

- No code or as much code as you want. The "no code" part is an absolute truth. You could drop a UI element in a scene and say - do something if these two things collide without writing any code! What's more, you could say things like - ensure it is a pixel perfect collision, or maybe wrapped them in a square, a bubble, a custom boundary… or use A* path finding out of the box for me please. My gosh, really?

- Finally, not to make this list too long, Game Maker demonstrated to me that I could write a game in days instead of months, if I just let go of the things that are not my natural skills and concentrate on the actual functionality I wanted - this is summarily huge!

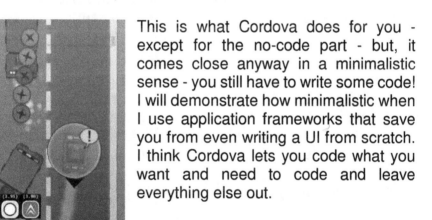

This is what Cordova does for you - except for the no-code part - but, it comes close anyway in a minimalistic sense - you still have to write some code! I will demonstrate how minimalistic when I use application frameworks that save you from even writing a UI from scratch. I think Cordova lets you code what you want and need to code and leave everything else out.

The Game Maker example represents another paradigm shift or iconoclastic statement (in a technology way). You must learn to let go of strict code structures and thoughts that if you did not write it then it is no good or, even that writing a lot of code is a good thing - it isn't and I hope I can demonstrate a lot of this here. I love writing code but I also love writing as little as possible and as much modular reusable code as I can to achieve my goals.

Ever since that day and since my experience with seeing Game Maker the first time, I ask my son for advice on a number of technical topics that want minimal complexity. The master is now the student!

Web development & Cordova

WebView and Invisible Browsers

As I mentioned earlier, given the technologies involved (HTML, CSS, JavaScript) writing a Cordova application is hardly any different from writing a web application. Of course, things can be very different and more or less complex depending on exactly which type of application you are writing (for instance, you cannot get the compass to work on a web application!) But for the most part, writing a Cordova app is very much the same.

The first thing you need to understand is that, unlike a native application that runs in its own memory space, a Cordova app runs in a browser. You do not see the browser because it is hidden behind the scenes but there are ways to show the browser window with menu and developer tools just like Chrome. But to preserve the spirit of everything encapsulated as a native application you simply do not see the browser window. For all practical purposes your application looks just like any other.

Most architectures refer to this hidden browser window as a WebView (IOS calls it a UIWebView and Windows calls it a Web View). The WebView is essentially a special browser - it could be a built-in browser that is being leveraged for this, a version of Chromium, IE or any other browser view. In other words, your application is behaving as a web page (or pages) running inside a hidden browser that makes it all look like a regular app.

Many people complain that there are some pretty intensive trade-offs in using a hidden browser window. For instance, as with any HTML page, you are required to define tags for **content security policies** which can get a bit complicated. Also, some people claim that performance of your app will be limited by how good the performance of the browser itself is. This is all true but fairly immaterial as you will see later when I talk about Hybrid vs Native Applications.

At the end of the day, the browser is invisible and your app looks no different than any other application. However, do be aware that your app is using web technologies to work (such as http requests, ajax calls, inline scripts possibly, etc.) This makes your app susceptible to web-based attacks such as cross domain calls and code injections. Admittedly, your app in the end is not a web page so it is harder to make these attacks on say an APK, but it is doable so consider all security protections that you would put on a web page and put them on the app as well.

If you are new to this field and you do not know what security protections are appropriate - do not worry. My worked out and real-life example will discuss and show you the most important details of this. In this section, I only want to highlight that you are indeed running inside of a browser so that you understand this concept.

Development Similarities and Differences

So, what are the similarities and differences between writing a web site and a Cordova App? Let us start by saying that a web site is not an app. The web site may be using very similar technologies but in the end, it runs on a server, not on a client or consumer device and it is less restricted to issues such as size, orientation, density, interaction with specific platform native code (such as magnetometer or speedometer), etc. You get the idea. If I am writing a compass application and I try to run that on the browser the application will work but the compass will not as there is no built-in compass on the web server.

The biggest similarities can be summarized as follows:

1. Your tools and knowledge in writing web sites ports 100% so if you are a web developer you already know how to make Cordova apps, you just need to make a couple of transitions but your tools will work fine;
2. If you are used to using application or UI frameworks like JQuery or Bootstrap (more on these later) they will work fine in Cordova - you simply need to be aware of a couple of minor concepts described below (such as waiting for a device-ready event) and you are set;
3. HTML scripting, JavaScript scripting and CSS are identical. Using a responsive design will go a long way to make sure your app behaves exactly as expected. Some additional CSS tags are commonly used for adapting to the device width or orientation but following responsive design procedures (for instance for a mobile website) will port without any issues;

The biggest differences can be summarized as follows:

1. You are running on a device that may be the size of a tablet (7" or so, perhaps 9" or 10") or the size of a smartphone (ranging from 4" to 6" or 7" or so). You cannot make assumptions about right absolute or fixed positioning easily as things may not fit on the screen or go off the screen. So, bear in mind you are not on a 17" screen;

2. Assets (images in particular) can be tricky to handle for every screen definition that there is. Specific elements like grids and tables may also be tricky as you can't assign sizes that would exceed the boundaries of the device. So, at all times you need to understand what the dimensions of the device are and ensure you do not blow past these. One trick that some use is to use the largest possible

image sizes and then scale them to the device. This works for the most part but you need to be mindful that a PNG file that is 4k square may take upwards of 100 mb of RAM thus crippling the performance of your app or the size of your package;

There are other differences but in my view, these are the most important ones.

Responsive Web Design

Since we talked above about responsive web design let's briefly visit this topic to understand what we mean by this. I am going to quote SmashingMagazine here for their definition of responsive design:

"Responsive Web design is the approach that suggests that design and development should respond to the user's behavior and environment based on screen size, platform and orientation. The practice consists of a mix of flexible grids and layouts, images and an intelligent use of CSS media queries."

So basically, when you design your UI using CSS directly or a CSS framework you have an option to specify how elements on the page behave and resize or scale depending on the dimensions or orientation of the device, among other things.

I mentioned in my introduction that this book is not designed to teach you how to program in JavaScript or CSS however, you can get great information from the source of these technologies. In the case of responsive CSS design, please read the following link for all the information that you need. Additionally, you will see examples of this in action in my Timer application below.

https://www.w3schools.com/html/html_responsive.asp

The article above explains in full detail what responsive web design is and why it matters and how to effectively design styles that are fully responsive and adaptive to any device surface.

Tools of the Trade: HTML, JS and CSS

As I mentioned above I am not trying to teach you how to program with HTML and JavaScript (JS) nor CSS but I want to highlight important concepts about these technologies and provide you with links to the best resources to learn them.

HTML and CSS will be your main technologies for designing the UI as well as page navigation. The UI is very critical to the user experience and there are many resources to learn more about the importance of good UI design. Here are a couple:

- **UI vs UX**
- **Learning CSS**
- **Learning HTML 5**
- **Learning JavaScript**

HTML determines the layout of the page or pages and allows you to construct your basic UI layout and behavior (such as for instance where to go when you click on a menu item, the design and implementation of the menu item itself and the addition of the necessary style sheets to format your interface). Here are some examples of HTML to give you an idea of what to expect. They are almost one-for-one the same as what you would do in a web page.

```
<html>
  <head>

        <meta http-equiv="content-type" content="text/html; charset=UTF-8" />
        <meta http-equiv="Content-Security-Policy" content="default-src 'self' data: gap:
            https://ssl.gstatic.com http://forecast.weather.gov 'unsafe-eval';
            style-src 'self' 'unsafe-inline'; media-src *">
        <meta name="viewport" content="user-scalable=no, initial-scale=1,
            maximum-scale=1, minimum-scale=1, width=device-width">

        <title>TideLock</title>

        <!-- TideLock references -->
        <link href="css/jquery.mobile-1.4.5.min.css" rel="stylesheet" />
        <link href="css/Madvox.min.css" rel="stylesheet" />
        <link href="css/colorPicker.css" rel="stylesheet" />
        <link href="css/index.css" rel="stylesheet" />
        <link href="css/label.css" rel="stylesheet" />

        <!-- Framework Scripts -->
        <script src="scripts/Frameworks/jquery-2.2.1.min.js"></script>
        <script src="scripts/Frameworks/jquery.mobile-1.4.5.min.js"></script>
        <script src="scripts/Frameworks/jquery.panzoom.min.js"></script>
        <script src="scripts/Frameworks/jquery.colorPicker.min.js"></script>

  </head>
```

Figure 1: Typical HTML Header Configuration

If you wish to use JQuery (or any other UI framework), as in fact I am doing in the example above - simply include the framework like you would do with any other web page and this should work. Further down I will go into more details about what you need to do to add UI and other frameworks and get them to work. The above figure is just an example of what HTML looks like in a Cordova page.

The example above does not contain the UI itself it is simply adding all require dependencies for using a UI framework (JQuery in this case) and its associated styles and scripts in preparation for starting the design which follows in the **body** section of the HTML file. More on this shortly.

Native vs Hybrid

A true non-issue

I have spent countless hours, days, months, researching the topic of Hybrid applications vs Native Applications. Before I get into any detail at all let me tell you something flat out - this is absolutely a

- Write Once Run Everywhere
- Gartner: >50% of apps are hybrid
- Cheaper and quicker
- Easy Writing and Design

- Complex. Needs rewrite per platform
- Faster
- More UX Centric
- Time Consuming
- Expensive

non-issue. Now let's delve into the details as to why this is so…

Native applications are built using dedicated tools that are made by OEM's (manufacturers of said tools) for the specific purpose of writing native applications (for instance, Android Studio, made by Google). Rarely can these tools do something other than helping you write a native application but there are indeed some tools (such as Eclipse, Visual Studio and Android Studio, among other) that can be used to write other kinds of applications (such as Cordova Apps). But the main purpose of these tools is typically to allow you to write a native application.

A native application is a binary executable (usually in the form of a package once all is built) that is specifically designed to run on a platform and no other. So, if you write a native application for Android using Android Studio, you will have access to all the cool tools and interfaces (such as for instance Material) that the platform has access to but if you try to install the application on a different platform (such as IOS or Windows) it will not work as it depends on functionality that is available exclusively to the native platform (Android in this case).

Therefore, if you write a weather application for Android using native tools and then you want that application to also run on, say, Windows Phone, you will need to rewrite it using Windows own native set of tools. So, if you want your app on three stores, say, you need three copies of the app usually written differently with different coding paradigms or languages (for instance, for Android Studio you will use JAVA; for Visual Studio C# and for XCode, Objective-c).

If you are entirely focused on a single platform and never expect to move your app to another platform (this is typically the case of corporations' line of business apps or larger enterprises) then you might as well use Native tools (not to say you can't use Hybrid tools) and take advantage of their UI and UX and all the tools they provide to native applications.

On the other hand, if you are trying to write the application and expose it to as many platforms as there are and not have to rewrite it for each single platform then use hybrid tools.

So, what is the catch here? How do you know if native is better than hybrid apart from the things stated above? It is very simple… Some people have perceptions that performance is bad on hybrid applications since they are not natively compiled executables and they run inside of a hidden browser which imposes an additional level of misdirection between your app and the operating system. This is strictly true but it has no practical implications.

It is true that a compiled binary native app responds quicker but this response may be completely immaterial depending on the type of app you are writing and, let me tell you right now, 99.9% of all apps out there simply do not care that much because their performance is perfectly acceptable, especially on the more modern devices.

So, when is it necessary to leave aside hybrid development and turn to native? A simple rule of thumb is this: do you need native functionality that is specific to the device or not available outside of that device capability? For instance, do you need to use a native material design that cannot be accurately or, performance-wise, reproduced outside of going native? If so, then do go native. Another example where performance can be an issue is certain sensors. I wrote a compass for a Cordova app and also for an Android Studio app. The performance of the compass is next to useless under Cordova and, like a real compass in Android so, for these native functions, going native maybe the best option.

For any other application that is using regular functions that are available everywhere, go hybrid and put your app in all stores, especially if you are a lone wolf or an indie developer and are not tied to a single OS infrastructure. For instance, apps like WhatsApp, Facebook, image collections, messaging, email, file managers and a very long list of apps of this type - your best option is hybrid so your app is available everywhere and there is no noticeable performance hit at all. If you aim to make a solar system simulation and need a load of graphical power such as it is provided by a native GPU then go native. These cases are very black and white which is why I say this is a non-issue; it is usually perfectly clear.

Aside from those considerations you should probably consider the following tips:

- Writing a native app is considerably more complex. Using HTML and JavaScript is very easy... wrapping your functionality in JAVA or C# classes, packages and modules is significantly more complex and it adds development time and/or cost to your project;

- Using hybrid tools like Cordova through long-standing standardized tools like HTML is not only easy but very fast. Designing your UI/UX without even writing any code yet is incredibly fast, affording you the chance to play with designs until you find what you like;

- The learning curve for JavaScript and HTML is significantly lower than C# or JAVA. Please note that I am an active programmer in those languages so I am not criticising - just acknowledging a fact.

Hopefully that clears up much of the fog around hybrid vs native apps.

Native tools

Let's examine a short list of very popular native tools. This are not by any means the only ones (I particularly like the Jetbrains IDE's and Eclipse) but they are arguably the most popular...

Xamarin and Visual Studio

These are two different tools but these days they come together since Microsoft acquired Xamarin (you can get them separately too if you want). I spent years waiting for this acquisition and asking Microsoft  why they weren't purchasing Xamarin. I kept asking because it was very obvious that Microsoft had absolutely nothing that was multiplatform and the Windows Mobile ecosystem was not doing very well at all so, writing your app just for Windows Phone and using pretty bad things like Win RT and later better tools like UWP (which never seemed to be finished) were just no options at all.

Xamarin on the other hand was an independent company that insisted on charging unaffordable prices for what was essentially Mono with some addons. You might say that eventually Xamarin lowered their prices but they were never affordable to Indies and you always were going to need the expensive business version if you really wanted to write a proper app.

One thing that Microsoft did that was absolutely perfect, after the acquisition, was to offer Visual Studio Community Edition for free with all these tools in it. The only thing you don't get in VS Community, as an indie, is all the things you don't care about anyway so this move by Microsoft was absolutely masterful.

I personally stopped using Visual Studio a while back despite it being my most favorite IDE. The reason is that it is a hulking mixture of stuff I love and stuff I don't want and it does not fit on my smaller SSD I use for development.

Ultimately, Visual Studio 2017 came out with a custom installer to help you reduce the footprint of the IDE. If you did not want Azure services or SQL you did not have to install them. Unfortunately, if you click on Cordova (TACO) tools it automatically checks another bunch of boxes (such as Windows SDKs and Windows 8 emulators) that you still do not want making the install size still 40 to 70 Gb. for a 125 Gb, hard disk it is just not acceptable to have such a footprint. The custom installer needs to be a lot more granular about this. I do not want 3 different Windows 10 SDK's and I can't seem to get rid of the ones I do not want.

Other than that, Xamarin under Visual Studio does provide the tools you need to write native apps for any platform. However, good as it is, I also do not use Xamarin even in its separate install form. The reasons are:

- Xamarin for Android requires you to write so close to Android native that frankly if you are just targeting Android it is far better to use Android Studio where you get what Xamarin offers and a lot more and integrated services from

Google as a bonus (you can publish your APK right from the IDE);

- If you are doing multiplatform (for instance Android and IOS together) then that eases things more but in the end, I find the shared UI (Xamarin Forms) not just quite there - as usual, it is easier to do things with the native tools for the specific platforms. Nevertheless, I can't argue that, if you make some sacrifices, you can use Xamarin for multiple platforms just fine so it is definitely a good tool;

- Overall, I find that Xamarin works if you want to invest the time and patience but all it buys you over a hybrid platform like Cordova, is native performance subject to my observations in the prior chapter and cross platform with Windows and IOS. That is very good so no complaints here, but it is not as easy as it seems and it has huge footprints so you better have a powerful computer (or at least a lot of storage space).

Android Studio

I absolutely love Android Studio even though it is nowhere as advanced as Visual Studio. Admittedly, Visual Studio can run circles around Android Studio yet I prefer Android studio these days (I've  used Visual Studio exclusively even before it was called InterDev!!). The reasons are quite simple:

```
File  Edit  View  Navigate  Code  Analyze  Refactor  Build  Run  Tools  VCS  Window  Help

package com.ntime.madvoxllc.ntime.Main;

import ...

public class MainActivity extends AppCompatActivity {

    private LinearLayoutManager DateLayout;
    private LinearLayoutManager TimeLayout;
    private LinearLayoutManager SparseLayout;

    private ViewPager viewPager = null;
    private PagerAdapter adapter = null;

    DrawerLayout androidDrawerLayout;
    ActionBarDrawerToggle actionBarDrawerToggle;
    NavigationView navigationView;
    Toolbar toolbar;
    ViewPager TabPager;
    TabLayout tabLayout;
    Tools AppTool = new Tools();
    DataHolder Holder = DataHolder.getInstance();

    public static MainActivity Instance;
```

- Footprint of 2 gigabytes or 5 if you install the NDK - this is versus 40, 60 or 80 gigabytes in Visual Studio - in other words, this works fantastically well in a small dev machine;

- It runs in Linux and other OS'. I use both Windows and Linux but lately mostly Linux for development. Xamarin and Visual Studio run only in Windows;

- It is fast, very fast - even the emulators are very fast compared to Windows - even on a small development laptop with 3Gb of RAM running Linux Mint - this thing is much faster than in Windows (my Windows machine dwarfs the Linux one by miles and miles - yet it is significantly slower with Android Studio);

- It has all the features you need and no more but also no less. Even code profilers and memory monitors are included. Visual Studio has that too but Android makes it so transparent and useful...;

- Free gets you everything - not that VS Community is bad because it isn't but Android is free and gets you everything you need - no future concerns about needing a professional edition or an enterprise edition of it;

- It is thoroughly integrated into Google Dashboard and Services so I can access those and do everything I need directly from the IDE. This is not the case with Visual Studio despite opportunities to do this easily.

XCode

I do not use XCode because I do not write applications for IOS. I could but I cannot get over the requirement of having to purchase a MAC to be able to build and deploy my app. This is no longer that much of a deterrent as there are companies that offer cloud builds (for instance Intel XDK) and so you can have a server build your app and you do not need a MAC. Nevertheless, I was never much into IOS development so I will not comment as extensively as I did earlier with other tools. XCode however does seem very nice and clean and at some point, I probably will use it.

Other IDE's

There are quite a lot of IDE's these days... the days of Microsoft having the only polished IDE are over. I will not list all the IDE's out there but these are the ones that I think are worth mentioning aside from the above...

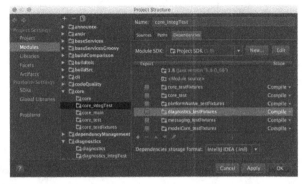

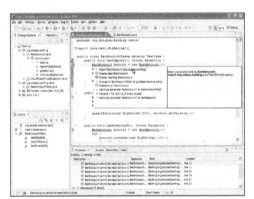

IDEA - it is basically the parent of Android Studio and it can do the same things plus full JAVA development (also Python and other) but it is not free so you need to pay for some features. IDEA can be used for Cordova Development.

Eclipse - another IDE that I have used extensively in the past but not anymore. It is however quite powerful and it has many plugins that do everything imaginable. It is free and it can be used for many languages, including C and C++, JAVA and others. It is a great IDE. Eclipse can be used for Cordova Development.

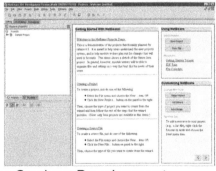

NetBeans - I used this IDE for writing midlets and small phone applications a long time ago.

Hybrid Tools

IDE's are powerhouses that integrate building tools, debugging tools, configuration, monitoring, performance and a myriad of other useful functions. But IDE's are not your main development tools. You will develop in a specific programming language and UI scripts which can be supported by an IDE or by any other editor (more on Editors below).

In the case of Cordova, you will be using JavaScript as your primary development tool (as well as HTML and CSS). Now, which flavor of JavaScript is entirely up to you - these days JavaScript simply does not come in a single flavor.

- You can use the basic standard JavaScript that comes out of the box supported by any IDE really. Just start writing JavaScript and you are good to go;
- You can use JavaScript application frameworks that provide additional abilities to the language for instance, to enhance the UI or to produce native code such as React JS by Facebook;
- You can use other application frameworks for JavaScript that focuse more on templating and code structure, for instance Angular JS or Ionic which is specifically written to work with Cordova;

Whichever you use (or none) you will be fine. I recommend using just JavaScript out of the box to get used to writing an app and then you can add Angular or Ionic to future projects if you wish to get more in-depth. Some of these frameworks also provide UI (CSS) elements preconfigured so you do not need to worry about writing your own widgets (such as calendar pickers or grids etc.)

I do have a strong recommendation for you although it is entirely optional. I personally use Typescript and I think if you did, you would not regret it. I use Typescript for a single reason - one and only reason - I cannot stand the lack of typing in Java - it simply confuses me, despite the fact that I consider it a great language.

But declaring every single variable as a global without regards to types and sometimes even scope, is too much for me. Therefore, I use Typescript which in the end does nothing but to output JavaScript anyway but the way you design your code is much cleaner than JavaScript alone.

By definition:

*"**Typescript** is a free and open-source programming language developed and maintained by Microsoft. It is a strict superset of JavaScript, and adds optional static typing and class-based object-oriented programming to the language."*

In other words, you can write Typescript which is JavaScript anyway, and have some code structure and types (for instance integers and strings and doubles) that just make things easier.
Here is a side-by-side comparison of Typescript vs pure JavaScript... remember that Typescript is optional - you do not have to use it:

```
function greeter(person: string) {
    return "Hello, " + person;
}

var user = "Jane User";

document.body.innerHTML = greeter(user);
```

Figure 2: JavaScript snippet/example

```
interface Person {
    firstName: string;
    lastName: string;
}

function greeter(person: Person) {
    return "Hello, " + person.firstName + " " + person.lastName;
}

var user = { firstName: "Jane", lastName: "User" };

document.body.innerHTML = greeter(user);
```

Figure 3: Typescript snippet/example equivalent to JavaScript above

```
var num = 1;
var str = '0';

// result is '10' not 1
var strTen = num + str;

// result is 20
var result = strTen * 2;
```

So, as you can see   there is a slightly elevated effort in setting up the Typescript but once you are done, the result is a very structured and type-sensitive JavaScript that will, optionally, make your life much easier as it will catch mismatches like this picture on the left...

The picture on the left is the main reason I do not like JavaScript as much as I could though still, I think it is a fantastic language.

UI Frameworks

Just like there are frameworks for JavaScript that help you write less and better code there are also frameworks for the User Interface. You will definitely appreciate and use these heavily as they save you tons of work and many hours of effort. There are many UI frameworks so I am only going to list here the two or three that are my preference and I consider the best. Some might disagree alleging that certain Frameworks such as JQuery are very big and add heavy weight to your application - while this is technically true the extra weight is well worth it and not that much of a drag on what you do but, if you think certain frameworks are too big you can certainly choose much smaller ones (like Bootstrap) though you may lose some useful functionality. It is your personal decision what to use. I will simply show you what is good to choose from…

JQuery: Recommended

JQuery has been around forever and it is one of the best known, best supported frameworks around. You simply cannot go wrong with JQuery. Some will correctly say that the developers of JQuery take years to update it - this is true and it bothers me as well. However, existing JQuery code is so very useful that it almost does not matter (it does though, do not get me wrong). JQuery is

also old in terms of years in existence and others like Bootstrap are far more modern and you may prefer them. I do prefer Bootstrap myself but I am too heavily invested in JQuery at the moment…

JQuery (which you can officially find **here**) comes in two flavors: JQuery and JQuery mobile. It is the mobile version you want to use for your projects as it has additional features that support touch and orientation, among other things.

JQuery Mobile provides code and plugins to help you set up a nice UI really quickly without having to mess with CSS (as JQuery does all that for you). JQuery is also responsive out of the box so it automatically adapts to all form factors, screen sizes and orientation. You can do all this yourself with CSS but why when JQuery has already done it for you? You can see how JQuery is set up and working in my example app further down.

JQuery has a true factory of so many plug-ins you can easily lose count. There is a plug in for everything so if you need zooming, pinching, animations, drawing, gadgets and widgets or anything else do not write it yet - go check the **JQuery Plugin Registry** because it is probably there for you.

Here are some examples of JQuery UI elements for you:

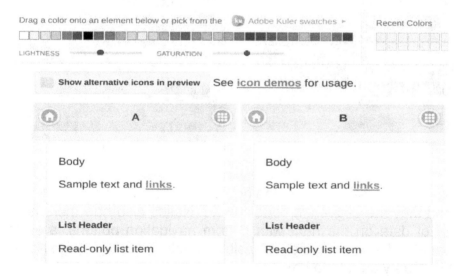

First of all, JQuery has a theme designing tool called the Theme Roller (which I use extensively) to select theming and colors for your apps (more than one if you wish). You can find the theme roller **here**.

To be sure: you can use this roller to create multiple themes and then allow the user to select one they prefer for your app.

JQuery has an incredibly rich set of functions. You may find them all in a demo here. A couple more screenshots below of what I personally have done with JQuery to give you an idea... These show you buttons, menus, grids, accordions, collapsible panels, etc....

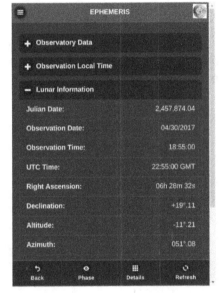

Notice how there is an image grid on the left, with image captions and they are aligned in certain ways. Notice also how there is a lot of data on the right with bottom navigation buttons, a side panel sliding button and collapsible panels. All of this is provided by JQuery out of the box.

Bootstrap: Recommended

Bootstrap is almost the same as JQuery except is far more modern and thus it may be more appealing in terms of a more modern look and interface. I really love Bootstrap and will be incorporating it into my UI soon. Bootstrap does work with JQuery so if there are parts of it you like but want to continue to use JQuery you can mix them with no conflict.

Being newer, Bootstrap does not have as many components, widgets and plugins as JQuery so you may struggle to find something important that you need. However, as mentioned above, you can provide a JQuery equivalent and mix them up together. This shortcoming is very small and it will not last as Bootstrap is possibly the most popular framework today (the way I see it). To see all that Bootstrap can offer look here. Some screenshots below…

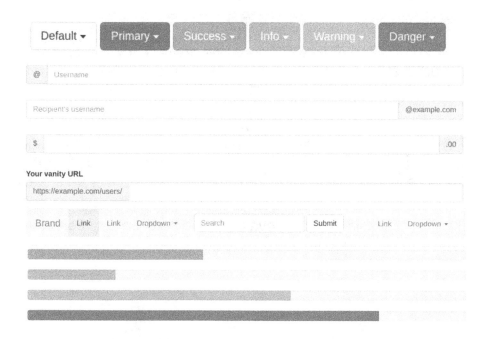

Other Interesting Frameworks

While the two above, to me, are the most important and favorites, there are many other frameworks that you may choose if you prefer what they look like or the flexibility they provide. Here are a few good ones you can look at:

- **Sencha Touch**
- **Ionic**
- **KickStart**
- **Kendo**
- **Material**

Cordova Tools

It is time to get to the meat of things now and talk about Cordova tools themselves. In this section, I will tell you what you need to do to understand Cordova from a practical viewpoint and to install everything you need and get going.

Versions and Releases

Over the course of time Cordova has made many versions and releases available. At the time of writing, I am using Cordova 6.5.0 as the latest stable version. By the time you read this, 7 or later will be out but this does not matter much with Cordova. You always want to be on the latest version if possible because of bug fixes or security patches or the like. Also, later versions usually have improved performance and more features so being in the latest version is a plus.

To view all versions of Cordova and the difference between them go to the official documentation located here.

Associated Tools

Cordova is a NodeJS application. What NodeJS is of no importance for this book but if you are interested, you may find everything you need to know about NodeJS here. Since Cordova is a NodeJS application and you are going to be writing Cordova Apps (not Node) it is not important to learn about Node right now.

Aside from IDE's and Editors (the latter will be discussed below) there is one more tool I want to cover now. This tool is a version control system which allows you to save your project every time you make changes so in the event of catastrophic loss or if you want to revert to earlier versions, you can keep track of that.

GIT Tutorial

There are many tools that can be used for versioning but my favorite tool is Git. Git is mostly a command console tool so in order to make your life easier and to use it through a graphical interface you may install a number of tools. I recommend SmartGit. I have used SmartGit for many years and it is an excellent tool.

Note that SmartGit is a commercial tool. There are a number of free Git UI Clients so feel free to choose others but I think SmartGit may be the best one around. SmartGit is free as long as you are not charging any money for your work. If you intend to charge, then you can purchase a cheap license of SmartGit and problem solved.

I want to show you a bit of how SmartGit is used because you will need to use a tool like it. The basic concepts of Git version management are:

- A repository: a folder on your computer or somewhere in the cloud where your file incremental changes will be stored so that you can later examine them or extract them;

- When you start development of your app you need to create a repository. This repository can be local to your computer, just for your personal use, or it can be placed anywhere on the network or cloud for access from different computers. You may also use GitHub if you plan to share your repository with others or ask for collaboration on your project. But if you are a lone wolf, you can just put it on your network drive or local computer which is what I do (I use a USB drive on the network and have access from multiple computers);

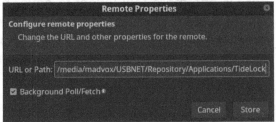

- If you are creating a repository on your local computer all you have to do is to add or create a repository from the file menu and just give it a name. If you want that repository to be shared on the network so that you can access it from other computers like I do, you need to create a "bare" repository on the network and link it to your local repository. To do this, open a command prompt and navigate to your network folder. Once there, issue the command "**git init --bare**". This will create a bare repository. Then return to SmartGit and go to REMOTE and PROPERTIES from the main menu. In the properties, enter the path of your network bare repository you just created. You are set to share your code with yourself over the network;

- Once you have done the above, you can add files to your repository. Since you have none so far,  just start your development and at periodic intervals, go back to SmartGit and "**stage**" new or changed files;

- When files are staged, they can then be **committed** to the repository. This saves a snapshot of the files so as you continue to change them, if you make a mistake, you can compare what is on your repository to what is on your machine and even get a copy back and undo any mistakes you made;

- If you are sharing the files on the network, after committing you may do a "**push**" which will send your local changes up to the 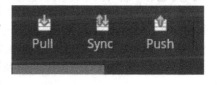 network so other machines can "**pull**" or retrieve them;

That is pretty much all I want to show you about git but I tell you, it is a life saver so use it. You do not have to do all this with SmartGit itself as most development tools, editors and IDE's are integrated with git so, as we will see below, you can add and stage files and even commit and push from the editors themselves.

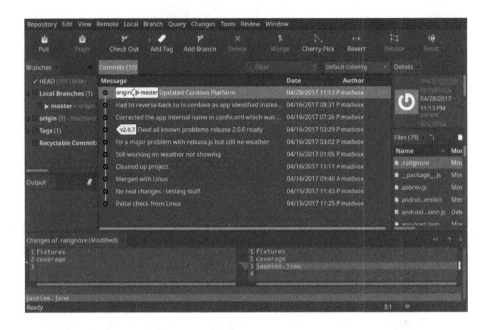

Cordova Installation and Dependencies

Before I show you how to install and set up Cordova let's make sure you are not missing other dependencies (tools that need to be installed before Cordova will work properly).

Windows Installer (.msi)

Windows Binary (.zip)

macOS Installer (.pkg)

macOS Binaries (.tar.gz)

Linux Binaries (x86/x64)

Linux Binaries (ARM)

Source Code

First of all, I mentioned earlier that Cordova runs as part of a framework called Node JS so you must do a one-time installation of Node JS before you can use Cordova. Node JS installation files are readily and easily available here.

To Install Node for Windows, Linux and MAC just download the appropriate file from the above link and double click it to install it.

In Linux (and also Windows if you use the ZIP option) you simply need to download the zip file and then extract it to a location of your choosing and put it on your path.

Preferred Method: In Linux (also in Windows) you can install Node manually by issuing the following command on an administrative console: **sudo apt-get install nodejs**. On Windows just run setup.

After you have installed Node JS you can issue the command **node -v** and if you get a response with a version number then you are set.

Once you have installed NODE JS you need to ensure you also have installed and updated the NodeJS Package Manager called **NPM**. This is part of node and remember, you are installing tools that are needed for Cordova to work but for practical purposes, you are just going through a laundry list right now - why you need these tools is not important to you right now - you simply need to install them for Cordova to work. So, make sure you have the latest version of NPM by issuing the following command on an administrative console: **sudo apt-get install npm** (on Windows just run setup for NodeJS).

To verify that NPM has installed properly issue the command **NPM -v** and if you get a version number then you are all set.

Now that you have node and npm installed you can install Cordova. To install Cordova, open an administrative command prompt or terminal and type the following: **npm install -g cordova**. When everything is done, type **cordova -v** and if you get a version number all went well.

To update cordova, npm or node at any time you simply repeat the commands above. While there are commands for updating these tools, the install command also serves as an updater.

Aside from the above, if you plan to write for Android or Windows or other platforms, there are additional tools to install. Personally, as far as you can, given that certain things run on Windows but not on Linux, I would try and install all dependencies so you can use a single development machine and deploy to any platform of your choice.

Platform dependencies needed (you need to install these) are as follows:

Java SE Development Kit 8u131

You must accept the Oracle Binary Code License Agreement for Java SE to download this software.

◯ Accept License Agreement ◉ Decline License Agreement

Product / File Description	File Size	Download
Linux ARM 32 Hard Float ABI	77.87 MB	⬇ jdk-8u131-linux-arm32-vfp-hflt.tar.gz
Linux ARM 64 Hard Float ABI	74.81 MB	⬇ jdk-8u131-linux-arm64-vfp-hflt.tar.gz
Linux x86	164.66 MB	⬇ jdk-8u131-linux-i586.rpm
Linux x86	179.39 MB	⬇ jdk-8u131-linux-i586.tar.gz
Linux x64	162.11 MB	⬇ jdk-8u131-linux-x64.rpm
Linux x64	176.95 MB	⬇ jdk-8u131-linux-x64.tar.gz
Mac OS X	226.57 MB	⬇ jdk-8u131-macosx-x64.dmg
Solaris SPARC 64-bit	139.79 MB	⬇ jdk-8u131-solaris-sparcv9.tar.Z
Solaris SPARC 64-bit	99.13 MB	⬇ jdk-8u131-solaris-sparcv9.tar.gz
Solaris x64	140.51 MB	⬇ jdk-8u131-solaris-x64.tar.Z
Solaris x64	96.96 MB	⬇ jdk-8u131-solaris-x64.tar.gz
Windows x86	191.22 MB	⬇ jdk-8u131-windows-i586.exe
Windows x64	198.03 MB	⬇ jdk-8u131-windows-x64.exe

For **Android,** you need to install a Java Development Kit (I use JDK 8 but 7 will do) and the Android SDK. You may install the Java SDK easily by downloading it from here and just installing it. From the list (shown above here) select the installer you need and download it. This is true for Windows too so install the Windows version instead if that is your operating system.

Note that on Windows, you can just open the installer and it will take care of everything. On Linux, you are downloading a zip file so extract it wherever you want and then set up some environment variables to make sure it is available to Cordova. The environment variables you need are these: (note it is recommended to unzip the JDK to **/opt/java**) ...

`JAVA_HOME=/opt/java/jdk1.8.0_45/`

If you installed the JDK in usr/java or another folder just replace it above to match your location. Also make sure you use the right JDK version (in here it is 1.8.0_45 but you may get a newer one). If you need more detailed instructions or do not know how to do this please consult this page for very detailed instructions and more help

In addition to the JDK you also need to install the Android SDK. Note that **if you install Android Studio it already installs the SDK and this is by far the easiest way to do this** so, even if you do not plan to use Android Studio I recommend downloading it and installing it from here and you are done!

If you prefer to just install the SDK manually then in Windows, you just need to download the SDK from here and run the setup program and you are done. In Linux though, first install a dependency for the SDK by opening a console with admin privileges and issue the command: **sudo apt-get install lib32ncurses5 lib32stdc++6**. After you have done that, install the Android SDK from here and then set up your environment variables like this:

Linux Install	Windows Install
• Install Node: **sudo apt-get install nodejs** and NPM: **sudo apt-get install**	• Install Node from Node SetUp
• Install Cordova: **npm install -g cordova**	• **NPM installs automatically**
• Install JDK **(use installer)**	• **Install Cordova:** from command prompt - **npm install cordova -g**
• Install Dependencies: **sudo apt-get install lib32ncurses5 lib32stdc++6**	• Install JDK from web site
• Install Android SDK: set**Use Installer**	• Install Android SDK from web site
• **Set Path:** export PATH="$HOME/Android/tools:$PATH" export PATH="$HOME/Android/platform-tools:$PATH	• No additional dependencies
	• No need to set path
	• **DONE**

```
export PATH="$HOME/Android/tools:$PATH"
export PATH="$HOME/Android/platform-tools:$PATH"
```

The Cordova CLI

CLI stands for Command Line Interface - in other words, things you type on a console or terminal (commands). Cordova has a CLI (a list of commands that you can issue on your project) and these commands are generally issued on a command console or terminal but do not worry… console commands are only needed to create or update projects and all of them can be issued within your chosen development tool so you do not really need to interface with the console if you do not like it. In this book, I will show you how to issue cordova commands from within your editors and in an automated way.

What commands does the CLI provide for you? Well, while you write your application you pretty much forget everything about Cordova since you are just writing your code. But when the time comes to check what you are writing, debug or test, you will need some commands to tell Cordova that you want in fact to do these things. So, Cordova has **build** commands, **release** commands, **sign** commands and others to help you accomplished these specific tasks.

I will show you how these commands work explicitly (if you want to use a console) or implicitly (inside of your own editor) in a few paragraphs below.

Development Environments

As I mentioned earlier, you may use any of the IDE's we reviewed above for Cordova development. However, I find that those IDE's are massive and they take a toll on your SSD or smaller development workstation. Some of them are not cross-platform either (such as Visual Studio) and thus you are stuck in one OS. If you are happy to stay on one OS then by all means use whatever IDE you like best. If you want to develop on any machine or OS then keep on reading this section.

I emphasize the toll that the IDE's take on smaller workstations because a lot of developers these days (such as myself) will use ultra-thin laptops with smaller hard disks like SSD 125 Gb and these IDE's will consume most of your disk space unnecessarily. I have a powerful laptop for certain things but 99.9% of the time I will be developing on my Linux ultra with only 4 Gb of RAM and a 125 Gb SSD and if I were to put a massive IDE on it I would cripple it needlessly, not to mention that I switch frequently between Linux and Windows so I need my tools to work on both OS'.

Personally, I think that instead of IDE's you should use a good editor and in my opinion, ATOM or Visual Studio Code are the best for this. I will focus here on Visual Studio code because it is not only impressive at what it can do but it is also new and they are constantly supporting it and adding features. But before we do that let's recap a bit...

Required Frameworks

Recall that you need a UI framework and for this you want to use JQuery or Bootstrap. As mentioned earlier there are many others so feel free to research and explore in case you like others better. Just remember that some of the frameworks that have been around longer or are more popular have many more features and you will need a lot of features.

Aside from the UI frameworks you may use code frameworks as well. I recommended Typescript because it helps you write scalable and organized code that is also strongly typed so you will make no mistakes by making everything a global variable and not being able to tell what is going on. There are additional frameworks like React-JS or Ionic or Angular and these are great but they require significantly more expertise to use. I recommend you stay with JavaScript and/or Typescript for now and graduate to other frameworks later as needed (if needed).

Finally, you need architectural frameworks that you do not necessarily need to understand but that are required by Cordova to work. We mentioned the Java SDK earlier and the Android SDK as well as Node JS and NPM. Those tools are required by Cordova so you can install them and then... forget them because for now they are not your concern at all. Assume they are simply needed for Cordova to function.

Non-IDE Editors

So, let's talk about Editors. Unlike IDE's which include everything above and under the rainbow, Editors include only what you need to be able to type and make a  program and nothing else. For a complex native application, I can see why you would use a powerful IDE that lets you examine your application as it runs and it displays performance and memory footprints. For hybrid applications, the performance and usage of the application is known beforehand as it behaves as you would expect in a browser and you could even use the browser to look into these things (Chrome has functionality similar to IDE's in that respect).

Editors like Visual Studio Code, ATOM, VIM, EMACS, Notepad++ and others are ideally suited for this job and here are some of the reasons why…

- An editor like ATOM or VSCODE has an absolutely minimal memory footprint so you can run them on powerful machines or the tiniest machines running XKFC and with very low specs. They will still run very, very well;

- An Editor storage footprint is also very small. VSCODE is just under 35 Mb and this is tiny for any system configuration. Granted you will add extensions and plugins but I doubt you would exceed 100 Mb when all is said and done. This is a great advantage on more compact systems;

- As a result of the two bullets above, editors perform like lightning. While an IDE may launch multiple threads, use up your memory and take forever to build and start debugging, an editor that has these capabilities will have none of those problems;

- One final reason: convenience, commodity, smallness, speed, simplicity and many more of those qualities are in abundance with these small editors. There is nothing you can do in your IDE (except things that do not matter that much) that you cannot do with ATOM or VSCODE.

And you get a much broader choice of editors. You like VIM, go ahead and use it. Notepad++, perfect for the job; you have total freedom here as long as, in addition to good editing, you can launch external commands so that we can build our projects.

One more note: what I mean by "good editing" is some features to make your life easier. If you just use Notepad you can write your app but its lack of features will make your life miserable. So, a good editor will have:

- Templating or snippets if you need help getting started;
- Syntax highlighting for the languages of your choice;
- Good project navigation into files and folders;
- Good structure for your project so you do not end up with a linear mess of files;
- Assistance to run external commands so you can use Cordova while in the editor;
- Good settings management for the editor and its environment;
- Good icons and color schemes so you can readily identify different components.

There is more but I consider the facilities above a "minimum must have" or else you do not have a good editor. Despite this though, you may be incredibly familiar with editors that do not do all these things and that is ok. At the end of the day this is more a matter of taste than a technical limitation.

Visual Studio Code

I am determined to teach you about Visual Studio Code for it is perhaps the most advanced and simplest editor you can use for this job and it is entirely worth using it. If you prefer other editors please feel free but I  am making a strong case for VS CODE here.

The first thing you need to notice is that the Visual Studio part of the name has absolutely nothing to do with the Visual Studio tool. VSCode was named this way, I assume, to keep the brand cohesive and also because VSCODE uses the same Monaco editor that the larger Visual Studio uses. Regardless, I want to make clear that VSCODE is not the same at all as Visual Studio, in fact, they could not be any more different. So, if you are expecting Visual Studio functionality you will not find it here.

So why VS CODE?

1. You need an editor anyway, it might as well be one of the best around;
2. It is fully integrated with GIT versioning systems;
3. It supports external tool integration so you can build, sign, debug and test within it;
4. It has templates, snippets and extensions to your mind's content;
5. It fully supports Apache Cordova in every possible way;
6. It has functionality that supports many other languages if you needed them;
7. It is fully cross-platform and it runs equally well in Windows, Linux or MACs;
8. It has linters, code formatters and many other useful tools that make your life easier;
9. It supports all kinds of build methods including Grunt and Gradle and MS Build;
10. It has perfectly excellent syntax highlighting, great grammar differentiation and settings customization.

There are other reasons but the 10 above are just impressive when taken all together. So, because of these reasons I have chosen VS CODE as the ultimate editor for this book and now I intend to give you a simple but good tutorial on it so we are on the same page as to how to use this tool.

Visual Studio Code (VSCODE) Tutorial

You can get VSCODE for your platform of choice **here**. Just go to the website, select your platform and download. Whether you are using Windows, Linux or MAC you can just run the installation program and this will simply work out of the box.

VSCODE, after installation, has all the tools you need except some extensions that we need to download to allow us to develop Cordova applications. Remember that Cordova and its prerequisites are already installed since we did that in earlier sections. Now, we need to install a couple of extensions to VSCODE to enable us to use those tools.

I will be covering these topics in more detail later but for now I want you to install these extensions so that we have a complete development environment. Other extensions and useful things can wait till later after I tell you what they are and how they work. So, I am skipping a little bit ahead for now just to complete the VSCODE setup.

After installation, VSCODE should look like the image below...

The bottom icon on the vertical navigator on the left is the extensions manager. Click that icon so we can install a couple of needs here... On the search box at the top type **Cordova** until you see the Cordova Tools and probably the Cordova Dev Essentials extension. We just need the Cordova Tools so click that and install it. After installation, you may need to reload the editor - if so, just click reload.

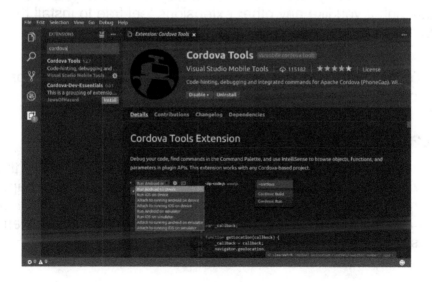

After you install the Cordova Tools extension, go ahead and type Chrome and choose the Debugger for Chrome so we can debug JavaScript in Chrome if we want to.

Finally, install TSLint (for Typescript) and also grab and install the VSCODE-ICONS which installs some nice icons for our different file and folder types. Once you have done this, you are set although if you like any other extensions feel free to install them but they are not needed for what we are working on.

Let's continue with our tutorial and break it down into some pieces...

Navigation

First things first - how do you use this thing? I am going to call this navigation. Click on the vertical menu on the two sheets of paper icon at the top. This section can collapse to make more room for your code so click it a few times so you can see how it opens and closes.

Notice that you have a top classic menu, a vertical menu bar with icons and a pink status bar which also has some important information we will discuss later.

VSCODE can open individual files or whole folders. Normally, you work with folders since your projects are made of many files and folders. There is no concept of a project or solution per se... folders are what matters so if you open the root folder of your project then that is, implicitly, your project or solution. To illustrate this, I will open up my TideLock application so you can see a full folder structure:

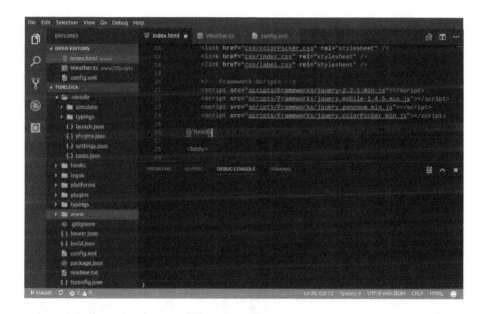

What you see above is the entirety of my TideLock application only some folders (such as www) are collapsed. There is a mixture of files here which I will explain later, right now I just want you to see the structure of a project which is folder-based. If you click on any folder on the left they will open and close as needed and, if you click on any file, it will be displayed in the main editing window. In the picture above I have split the view so you can also see a control window under the editor window, which allows me to debug or open up a terminal as needed. You can split windows in VSCODE in many ways, including having more than one source file open at the same time side by side or you may use tabs to navigate between files.

Note that VSCODE uses an internal management system for displaying files whereby if you single click on a file it shows it in the editor as a preview but if you click on another file it does not open another tab it simply shows you a preview of that other file. If you want to keep files (more than one) open, double click the file so a tab is pinned to the editor and now if you click another file, this one will remain open. Or if you edit or make changes to a file it also stays open.

VSCODE when closed, saves files you have not saved in a temporary folder so you never lose your work if you accidentally close the editor or the power goes out. But eventually you need to click SAVE to keep your file structure up to date in the right folders. Of course, running or debugging your app automatically saves all changed files.

Extensions

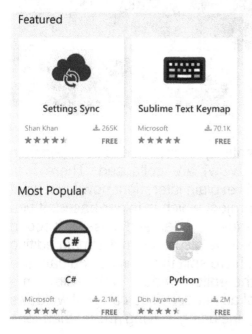

I already forced you to install an extension before you had a chance to read this section but let's examine extensions a bit more closely.

Extensions are like plugins that extend the functionality of the editor. VSCODE has an extension **marketplace** that can be browsed on the web or from this extension manager directly.

It is easier to use that link and browse extensions on

the web to see much more detail about them but ultimately, the extension manager in VSCODE is a much more convenient way to install the extensions you want.

If you click an extension once a window displays all relevant information that you need to know about said extension.

VSCODE lets you write extensions. This is a topic for a different day but know that many people write useful extensions that you might be interested in such as new color schemes and themes or code snippets and templates on how to write apps and many other useful things so feel free to browse and install whatever you need or like.

I use VSCODE for more than just Cordova development so I have extensions for .NET Core, C#, C++ and many more.

Preferences

Preferences may be important or not depending on what you want. For me, preferences are not very important in that I just use most of the defaults and that works fine for me. But VSCODE allows you to change user settings and workspace preferences and it has a very deep and broad catalog of settings you can change. One of the settings I find particularly useful is to hide files that are generated by intermediate processes so I do not have to see them cluttering my view.

The **Files Exclude** setting hides unneeded JS and MAP files from their Typescript equivalents which I really do not need to see.

Terminal

VSCODE comes with a built-in terminal or command window. At first this may appear not very useful but in fact, it is extremely useful

especially if you use the Cordova CLI as it saves you from opening a separate terminal just for that job. You may issue external commands just from this terminal at any time. You may realize you are using an older version of Cordova and just update from right here. Or you may have been working on an Android version of your project and have decided to add an IOS platform as well and you can do that from right here. I will show you more CLI commands and how to issue them from this window soon.

Git Integration

I mentioned before that VSCODE is integrated with GIT. You may use SmartGit for specific tasks but adding new or changed files, staging, committing and such can be done from right here. In the example image I showed you above I did not have any files that needed to be staged or committed but examine the image below, where I changed one file, so you can see what happens…

As you can see I inserted a space in the settings.json file and VSCODE immediately noticed this. I could now click the checkmark above to the left to stage or add this file and I could enter a commit message and commit the changes to the repository directly from here. If, as I described earlier, you have a network repository you will also need to push the changes to it. VSCODE does not do the pushing as far as I know but you can do this with SmartGit when needed.

Project Structure

Let us now examine what a project is made of. When you saw the image above you saw a lot of folders and files. Some of these are automatically created by either VSCODE or by Cordova but some are created by me to help me organize files so, I want to show you default folders that are created by the tool and are strictly needed and the ones I create which you may create differently to suit your needs.

Folder Hierarchy

.VSCODE

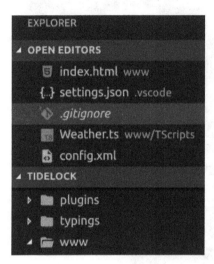

This folder is created when you first create or open a folder with VSCODE and it contains files that are special to VSCODE. This may include simulation files, typings for Typescript, and a variety of other auto-created files or folders. If you see new files and folders here that you did not create or edit, assume that those are created automatically by VSCODE and must not be messed with. In reality, if you accidentally delete these files they will be re-created on the next build but still, best to leave them alone if you do not understand what they do or what they are for.

Other files in this folder, typically with the extension JSON are created for you but you do need to work with them. You may assume that JSON files are yours and you can edit them.

There are various types of JSON files that are used to aid you in building, packaging and releasing your project. They are described in detail below.

WWW

This is a critical folder. It is created by Cordova when you first create an application (examples below) and it is the main folder you will do your work in. It typically contains a CSS folder for style sheets, a Script folder for your JavaScript, an Images folder for your assets and an Index.HTML file which is the landing page of your application. There may be more folders and files here that I have added but the ones I listed above are automatically created for you. However, the WWW folder is yours and you are free to delete those folders, rename them or add new ones at will. Cordova will pick up whatever is there and bundle it into the app. The one file that must exist and be named is **index.html**. You will also need a **config.xml** file in the root and we will examine that in a short bit.

I tend to add a TScripts folder where I store the Typescript files to separate them for my normal JavaScript. I also tend to add a fonts folder if I am using non-default fonts and a library folder for any external code that is not mine. There is also a **GITIgnore** file there which helps you tell git which files you do not need tracked.

Eliminating files that you do not need tracking for is important because as you build your project many intermediate, binary and large files are created that are temporary and they change every time you build. If you stage or add these files your repository will become needlessly big and cumbersome. Here is an example GITIgnore file that eliminates most of what is not wanted (as a general rule of thumb you should track only your source code or files you create or edit and not temporary files that are created as a result of normally building your project).

This ignore file is telling the system to not track the files you see. The [Pp] means it does not care about case for the word Plugins or Platforms. GITIgnore can take quite a number of parameters so feel free to look at other examples or at the git documentation. For example, a useful rule is to say:

!www

/.*

This means do track (do not exclude) the www folder but do not track anything else at all! So, there are many ways to accomplish the same thing thus, read the GITIgnore configuration from the git documentation to see what suits you best. In the end, what you are trying to do is not track irrelevant files that may make your repository big and clumsy for no reason.

Config.XML

This is a critical configuration file created by Cordova. You will need to make adjustments to it as you go. The importance of this file is as follows:

- It is the main Cordova configuration file that specifies the name of your application and additional data about yourself;

- It is an interface to a manifest which is required by most platforms. In Cordova, you do not edit the AppManifest.xml file, for instance; instead you enter information in config.xml that modifies the manifest when it is built. It contains references to key assets such as splash screens or application icons;

- The file also contains a definition of all the plugins you are going to use so they get included in the build;

- Finally, the file contains special customizations and platform values that you can edit such as the name of your app as it will appear in the store, different configurations for Windows, Android and IOS etc.

I will be giving you a good example of a config.xml file from my applications in the stores so you can get a good roundup of what you need to alter here.

Platforms

Platforms are critical as they specify which target operating system you want your application to run on. Because of this, I will take a bit of time now covering what platforms are and why they are important, including describing the three major platforms in some detail. If you want to take a quick look at all available platforms they are listed in the official Cordova site.

	android	blackberry10	ios	Ubuntu	wp8 (Windows Phone 8)	windows (8.1, 10, Phone 8.1)	OS X
cordova CLI	✓ Mac, Windows, Linux	✓ Mac, Windows, Linux	✓ Mac	✓ Ubuntu	✓ Windows	✓	✓ Mac
Embedded WebView	✓ (see details)	✗	✓ (see details)	✓	✗	✗	✓
Plugin Interface	✓ (see details)	✓ (see details)	✓ (see details)	✓	✓ (see details)	✓	✓

Platform Requirements

Each platform may be configured slightly different depending on what you want to achieve. Some configuration elements are required by each platform but these are not many. Primarily you configure a platform simply to suit your needs and in my examples below you will learn how to do this. In this section I am going to list only required settings besides your own.

Android

For Android, you just need to make sure the JDK and the SDK are installed and we showed you how to do this in earlier sections so you should be all set. Aside from this requirement you may modify the config.xml file to specify the following:

- Application version code and store version code;
- Minimum Android SDK version which determines which devices your app works on;
- Target SDK version - the version of Android you are specifically targeting;
- Android Assets (splash screen, icons and app images);

Windows

For windows, you need Windows 8 or Windows 10 as your base operating system and you also need the JDK and the Android SDK installed which you did in earlier sections so provided you have Windows 8 or 10 you are set to go.

Additionally, you may also change config.xml for the following Windows optional settings:

- Application version code and store version code;
- Windows Assets (splash screen, icons and app images);
- Target Windows Version if needed;

IOS

For IOS you also need the JDK and the SDK as well as XCode tools which you should have installed earlier. Additionally, you may alter config.xml for the following:

- Application version code and store version code;
- IOS Assets (splash screen, icons and app images);

Desktop Platforms

You may build and run Cordova applications on the Windows and Linux desktops as well as on the Chrome Browser. For Windows, the application can be built as a desktop app and it will run similarly to a UWP or Windows Store Application.

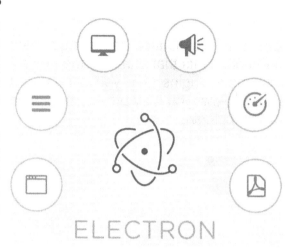

ELECTRON

For Linux, you need to use the Electron framework to enable the app to run as a Linux Image. This is actually very simple to do - it consists of modifying essentially two lines of code and so I will show you how to do this in the appendix.

I do not work with MACs so I am not including information here on how to run the application on the MAC. Please, refer to Apple's documentation for that additional information.

Note that although you are running the applications on desktops they are still mobile applications and they will behave as such. If you used responsive design the applications will look perfectly fine and just like any other desktop app. However, functionality that is specific to a mobile device will not work (for instance compass or orientation) unless your desktop device has such capabilities (some Microsoft Tablets can be run in desktop mode and have said capabilities but most other desktops will not be able to do this and my recommendation is that for a desktop release, you make a branch in git and strip mobile-specific components from your app and menus).

Plugins

Cordova, like JQuery, has a large selection of plugins which are code elements that enhance the functionality of your application. The main plugins (and you will use at least some of these) are listed below (you may browse the repository containing upwards of 2000 plugins here):

▼ Core Plugins

	NAME	VERSION	PLATFORM
☑	Battery	0.2.4	Android/iOS/WP8
☑	Camera	0.2.4	Android/iOS/WP8
☑	Capture	0.2.4	Android/iOS/WP8
☑	Console	0.2.4	iOS/WP8
☑	Contacts	0.2.5	Android/iOS/WP8
☑	Device	0.2.4	Android/iOS/WP8
☑	Device Motion	0.2.3	Android/iOS/WP8
☑	Device Orientation	0.3.2	Android/iOS/WP8
☑	File	0.2.5	Android/iOS/WP8

Further down I will show you how to install and configure plugins for your application. For now, be aware that plugins provide excellent functionality (native in many cases) that you will need.

Languages and Scripts

We are starting to approach the melting point of this document now. Bear with me a little bit longer while I finish introducing you to every concept you need to know or be aware of but we are very close now to writing an app. In fact, I am going to start introducing you to it in this very chapter and we will speed up towards a detailed working example.

Recap for now that in order to become familiar with Cordova and to be able to write an application you need to:

- Install Cordova as described above;
- Have some familiarity and learn HTML since this is your main design tool;
- Have some familiarity with CSS but no need to go deep since UI frameworks help here;
- Have some familiarity and ultimately learn deeply about JavaScript;
- Optionally, learn Typescript but this is not immediately needed at all;
- Learn how to use the Cordova CLI to compile, build and debug your applications;
- Learn an editor like VS CODE to use great features to type in and write your app.

That seems like a long list but the real hard part is to learn JavaScript but with a few examples, the references I have provided above and one step at a time, you will get there soon.

HTML

HTML together with JavaScript are going to be your bread and butter. Although I will not be teaching you HTML here (refer to learning resources I provided above or in the appendix), I will be talking about HTML. If you get confused because you do not understand HTML please do take a tour of the learning resources then come back right here because I will assume you have done that.

HTML or Hypertext Mark-up Language is a scripting language that uses a series of tags (opening and closing tags) to encapsulate design functionality used to build a web page. Typically, HTML consists of a header and a body. The header contains information useful to devices and service providers regarding how the application work - for instance, the header may contain tags indicating how security is to be applied to the site or who is the author, title and information such as that. Finally, the header is also the place where you can include your CSS stylesheets which shape up what your screen looks like. At the very least (and usually you can just get away with this), you will include a CSS style sheet for your chosen UI framework and that will take care of everything for you.

For instance, I use JQuery in my examples so there will be a link to a JQuery stylesheet that defines what my application looks like in terms of fonts and colors and things like that and that is all I need.

Aside from the stylesheets, the header is also typically the place where you place reference to the JavaScript that will be used in your HTML. While HTML is a tool for formatting your pages and CSS is a tool for giving those pages a look and feel, JavaScript is your code. You will be providing the functionality of your application using JavaScript.

To make that clear…

- HTML represents the structure of your application (whether it has menus, text fields, input fields, etc.);
- CSS represents what your application looks like (font, colors, sizes, things like that);
- JavaScript is where you write the functionality of your app. If an HTML field requires a number input, you can use JavaScript to read that input and see if it is valid, for instance.

Blank Cordova Template

So where do we start then? How do we get an application going? This is the section where I teach you that. We will create a very small, empty application that just says "hello" to you in order to illustrate what a skeleton template for an application should look like.

Here is what is required (aside from having Cordova and VS CODE installed):

1. Creating a project with Cordova which we can then open in VS CODE;
2. Adding one or more platforms to the project (Android, Windows, etc.);
3. Adding one or more Plugins if you need them (more on this soon);
4. A file called INDEX.HTML which is our starting point for the application;
5. A file called CONFIG.XML which contains information about what the app needs;
6. Your style sheets and/or UI Frameworks (we will use JQuery);
7. Your JavaScript to provide functionality;
8. If you are going to use version control (optional) we will create a repository as well.

We can proceed in order to create all these things so let's get started.

Creating a Cordova Project (empty)

For now, we will do this manually using the Cordova CLI. Later I will show you how to automate these CLI tasks so you do not have to do this manually but for now, it is a good idea to understand the CLI…

Go to some place in your computer, wherever you want, and create a new folder for your application. For now, I am going to call this folder simply "test". So, create the "test" folder anywhere you want.

Now, right click that folder and select to open it with VS CODE. VSCODE will open the folder and it will be empty except for .vscode which is a folder added automatically by the editor. You may ignore what is in there for now; we will come back to it later.

Now, access the VSCODE terminal by clicking on it and issue the following command:

cordova create TestApp

Be careful of some operating systems like Linux that are case sensitive so Cordova and cordova are not the same thing. Capitalize as needed but issue all commands in lowercase just to be safe.

Press enter and you should see a prompt indicating that cordova is creating or has created the project TestApp. This will be our project name - TestApp. If you browse the folder now you will see that Cordova created a few folders of its own. You can see this on VSCODE itself; TestApp has popped up in the editor and you can see a few folders underneath it. These are created by Cordova and you need them all so do not delete them. In time, we will edit CONFIG.XML and the contents of WWW but for now, just take it all in slowly.

So, we have a new project called TestApp in a folder called "**test**" but we have not told Cordova what platforms we want our project (or app) to run in. So now is the time to tell it that. To add a platform (or many) you need to issue a command to create said platform. Let's target Android… issue the following command from the terminal:

cordova platform add android

When this command finishes, a new folder is added to TestApp and this is our android target. If you add more platforms (say Windows or IOS) new folders will be created under "**platforms**" for those targets. For now, we will stay with Android. Let's take a look at what things look like so far. Your screen should look like this:

So, we have created a folder to hold our project or projects (remember a project is a folder in Cordova so the TestApp folder is really our project together with everything that is inside it), we created the TestApp folder through Cordova and we added an Android platform which means that as of right now our app will generate an APK file which is the package that runs on Android. Let's try this out…

Issue the following command to simply run the application you just created. We will be running the app in much better ways later but for now just do this:

cordova run

APACHE CORDOVA

.... from the terminal and watch the application being built. Since you have not configured any defaults in VSCODE yet the application does not know where to run, it only knows it is an Android app from the platform we added so it will start up an Android emulator from the Android SDK.

By the way, if you did not install Cordova correctly, you will get errors and the application will not run so refer back to the installation chapter and make sure everything is ok and try again. Here is a screenshot of what you should see (left)...

That was easy, wasn't it? We are only just getting started but you have created your first application using Cordova and it runs on Android pretty well. This is a default application created by Cordova to give you a starting point. Before we move on, let's examine it a bit close...

Cordova has created for you an Index.html file and a Config.xml file and this is all you need for now to run this simple application. Notable things:

- Index.html is very simple... it defines a default head with some basic tags that we will cover later and a simple stylesheet (feel free to look at these). The HTML tells the app where to put things on the screen and the CSS tells the app what these things should look like;

- The Config.XML file describes what this application is, what it does and a number of assets (images) that are needed for icons and such things. It is filled by default so please take a look at config.xml and see where you need to make changes. I'll bet it is almost self-explanatory. For instance, widget id is your app name so you could change that from the default io.cordova.hellocordova to say, TestApp or more customarily, list your domain and your app name like com.yourcompanyorname.TestApp - this is a typical way to name app packages.

You can continue to glance inside of config.xml and find that you need to provide a version number, your name, your email etc. These are basic things. We will cover the more complex ones later.

If you look inside the Platforms folders and then on to android/build/outputs/apk you will see an APK file there called android-debug.apk - this is your app… you could right now move it to an Android device and it will work but let's not do that yet… I still need to show you how to properly assemble an app this is all just default stuff but I am highlighting that it works out of the box.

Summarizing…. These are the commands you issued:

- Make a folder somewhere and call it **test**;
- cordova create TestApp
- cordova platform add android
- cordova run

Notable observations:

- Cordova must be installed first;
- Android SDK also needs to be installed. An emulator will pop when you issue the **cordova run** command. This emulator can be changed by choosing a default in the Android AVD manager (installed with the Android SDK).

Page Structure and navigation

Let's revisit Index.html to explain an important concept when writing hybrid applications. It is important that you understand the page model used by the application. For a comprehensive list of concepts on this topic please visit a resource such as **JQuery Pages**.

A page is a unit of activity in your application. Imagine you are building a Moon Phase and Calendar application. Your application entry page could be a cover page with an icon for moon phase and an icon for a monthly calendar. Further, if you click on the phase icon, you will be taken to another page that shows the moon phase and, if you click on a calendar, you will be taken to a page with a calendar which is different from the phase page. Look below for an example of pages from my application TideLock…

The illustrations above represent three different pages in the application. You may be inclined to think right away that a single

page is equivalent to a single HTML file and, you would be mostly correct. However, there are different ways to create pages in HTML. Let's discuss this…

Single Page Architecture

In this school of thought, INDEX.HTML is it and all your pages will be defined here. Different UI frameworks have different ways to define a page but since we are using JQuery, I will use that to construct pages. You can check the Bootstrap documentation (very similar anyway) or other UI frameworks for how they want you to build pages.

So, in other words, JQuery allows you to have a single HTML file and you can define all your pages inside of it by using a meta tag that declares a section of INDEX.HTML as a page. Here is an example:

```html
<!-- Entry Page -->
<div     data-role="page"     data-theme="a"     data-title="TideLock" id="index" style="background-image:
url(images/backdrop.png);">
  <div data-role="header">
    <h1 id="INTitle1">T I D E L O C K</h1>
    <a    href="#MenuPanel"    data-icon="bars"    data-iconpos="notext">Menu</a>
    <img         src="n.png"         class="ui-btn-right"
style="height: 32px; width: 32px;" />
  <div>
   <div data-role="content">
     <div style="text-align: center">
        …..
     <div>
   <div>
<div>


<-- Moon Phase Page -->
<div     data-role="page"     data-theme="a"     data-title="Phases" id="WLPhase">
   <div data-role="header">
      <h1>MOON PHASE</h1>
      <a    href="#MenuPanel"    data-icon="bars"    data-iconpos="notext">Menu</a>
```

```
        <img                        src="p.png"
style="height:32px;width:32px;" />
   <div>


   <div data-role="content" style="background-color:
#000;">
      <div id="LPhase">
         <div       data-role="collapsible"       data-
collapsed="false">

             …..
         </div>
      </div>
   </div>


<!-- Moon Calendar Page -->
<div       data-role="page"       data-theme="a"       data-
title="Poster" id="WLPoster">
   <div data-role="header">
      <h1><span id="PMonthHead"></span></h1>
      <a   href="#MenuPanel"   data-icon="bars"   data-
iconpos="notext">Menu</a>
         <img        src="m.png"        class="ui-btn-right"
style="height:32px;width:32px;" />
   </div>


   <div data-role="content" style="background-color:
#000;">

      …..
   <div>
</div>
```

The above three code snippets have been stripped of a lot more
tags where the "….." are placed. This is just to simplify so I can
show you what pages look like in the Single Page Architecture -
all of them built inside of INDEX.HTML so you have a single
HTML page with multiple pages within.

The key to this model is that you use tags to define what a page is. In the case of JQuery, we are using the **<DIV DATA-ROLE="PAGE">** to say "this is the beginning of a single page" and then the **<DIV DATA-ROLE="HEADER">** to define the headline title of the page and finally, the **<DIV DATA-ROLE="CONTENT">** to specify that this is what the page contains. We can use those tags to enclose multiple pages.

Multi-Page Architecture

The other school of thought is called Multi-Page architecture or MPA. in this case, each page goes into its own HTML file so you do not have to use those DATA-ROLE tags and, you will end up with one HTML file for every page you make.

Starting with INDEX.HTML, perhaps containing your main menu, when you click on a menu icon (such as Moon Phase) a page containing that will be linked (perhaps a page named MoonPhase.HTML). So, in this case, you have as many HTML files as you need to, one per page, and perhaps that way you can organize your code better.

The system uses something call AJAX calls to bring in every new page from within the HTML file. You do not need to be concerned for the purposes of this book, on how AJAX works but you should know that AJAX is a mechanism used by servers to serve pages to clients (apps) without refreshing the page and that AJAX thus introduces an indirection (additional steps) to find and load your page. The more pages you have the more noticeable (slow) things could get.

SAP or MPA - Which Works Best?

So, should you use Single Pages inside of INDEX.HTML and have just a single HTML file or should you have multiple ones, one per page? This is entirely a matter of taste or a design decision you make freely. There are some pros and cons but they are very basic. Let me illustrate the most important considerations:

SPA
- There is only a single INDEX.HTML file making your folders smaller and cleaner;
- You do not need to worry about where things are as they are all inside INDEX.HTML;
- The file can get very big if you have many pages and a big INDEX.HTML can slow the app down;
- There is no AJAX call to load pages so this is quicker than an MPA equivalent version.

MPA
- Much easier to organize code in pages if you have lots of pages;
- If you create many pages your folders will contain more files obviously;
- You need to separate pages logically so you do not mix functionality from other pages;
- AJAX will be used to find and load pages. If there are many, your app may be slower;
- Much easier to structure and organize things when functionality is in its own pages.

You make the call. Read the JQuery Page resource above for more clarity and see what you like.

Cascading Style Sheets (CSS)

Stylesheets, as mentioned several times, define what your application looks like. There are entire manuals devoted to CSS so it is a broad subject but I am telling you right now, especially for the purposes of this guide, you do not need to delve too deeply into CSS until you are comfortable because, if you are using a UI framework like JQuery - this framework already provides CSS files that it uses automatically and you can use some minor modifications to adjust it to your preferences (as opposed to writing a CSS for your project from scratch).

I will use TideLock again to illustrate how I am using the JQuery stylesheets. Stylesheets are added to INDEX.HTML in the **HEAD** section like this:

```
<!-- TideLock references -->
<link href="css/jquery.mobile-1.4.5.min.css" rel="stylesheet" />
<link href="css/Madvox.min.css" rel="stylesheet" />
<link href="css/colorPicker.css" rel="stylesheet" />
<link href="css/index.css" rel="stylesheet" />
<link href="css/label.css" rel="stylesheet" />
```

The style sheet you need to include for JQuery to work is the **css/jquery.mobile-1.4.5.min.css**. **css/** refers to the folder, within the current folder, where the file is located. So, this will look to add the css file from TideLock/www/css since INDEX.HTML is inside of WWW.

```
.TitleText {
    font-size: 20px;
    text-align: center;
}

.SubTitleText {
    font-size: 12px;
    text-align: center;
}

.event {
    border-radius: 4px;
    -webkit-border-radius: 4px;
    color: #FFFFFF;
    margin: 27px;
    padding: 4px 0px;
    text-transform: uppercase;
    background-color: #696969;
    animation: fade 3000ms infinite;
    -webkit-animation: fade 3000ms infinite;
}
```

As you can see, I added a number of other stylesheets. This is because I have a few pages that do not rely on JQuery but my own devices and so I have some special styles defined for those pages contained in Madvox.min.css. I also made an index.css that contains theme roller themes for JQuery so the user can select them and also a color picker etc. But you only need the jquery.mobile css to get going so you may safely ignore my other CSS examples given above.

What does a CSS file look like? Here is an example above. You can see that it contains definitions for different classes and properties of the former such as colors, backgrounds, images, sizes, etc.

A class, as I have just called it, starts with a dot ("."') and you can specify a **class** attribute to an HTML tag and it will use the styles defined in that class so, for instance, in the image above I have a class called TitleText which defines a font of 20 pixels and a center alignment. If I write an HTML tag like this…

```
<label class="TitleText">Hi there</label>
```

The words "Hi there" will be printed on the screen, centered and with a font size of 20 pixels because that is what the **class** tag is telling this label to do. HTML puts a label on the screen and the class tells HTML how to format that label.

There is obviously a lot more to it than I am letting you see but these are the basics. To learn more about CSS use the **this learning resource**. Alternatively, for now, skip it and rely on the JQuery CSS to do the work for you automatically.

Note that throughout this book I am not encouraging you to ignore CSS or any other technology. I am simply saying that, because I am not teaching you these technologies, I am giving you resources to go and learn at your leisure or, ignore that for now and rely on defaults. But ultimately, to have full control and understanding on how the application is functioning, you will need to learn more about these technologies. I will simply leave the development of more in-depth expertise to you and your time commitment.

Typescript

I mentioned Typescript (TS for short) a few times in earlier chapters. Let me recap why I mentioned it…

TS is an optional superset of JavaScript. It was designed to overcome some gaps in JavaScript (some would not agree to calling these gaps and I can sympathize). An example such gap, if you wish to call it that, is that JavaScript is not a "strongly typed language". What that means is that when you define a variable in JavaScript like so:

var i = 0;

This variable can be anything you want. For instance, I just said above "declare a variable, name it i and assign it the value 0". This may make you assume that i is an integer but it isn't - it is an **object** variable that is holding the value 0. But several lines below I could say:

i = "hello";

And now i contains the value "hello" and not 0 anymore.

For most people, especially deep fans of JavaScript, this if phenomenal - so much freedom to do what you want. I can sympathize with that honestly, I like that too. But there is a problem. What if I do this…

```
var i = 1;
var a = '0';
var b = i + a;
var c = b * 2;
```

Two questions for you…

What is the value of b? What is the value of c?

For b, if you answered anything other than "10" you were wrong. The value of b is 10. For c, if you answered anything other than "20" you are again wrong. The value of c is "20". How does this happen? What did you expect?

I tell you what I expect coming from languages like C++, Java, C#, etc.... I expect that the third statement (i+a) would result in an error as you cannot add a string or char and an integer. Second, I expect the fourth statement to yield c with a value of 0, null or undefined because b cannot be computed for the reasons I just said. But JavaScript yields 20 with no errors whatsoever and no compiler warnings that you are trying to add apples and oranges. Why?

Because JavaScript is designed to do this and I do see the great, great value in it. Recently I was trying to convert my TideLock application from JavaScript to JAVA and I gave up because I use many arrays that are a mix of integers, floats, doubles and strings and JavaScript is ok with that whereas JAVA will bite you for it, as it should. These are different languages designed to do different things.

JavaScript is doing some internal translations and assuming for you that if you are adding a number to a string and the string contains a number in it then these two things can be added - it implicitly converted '0' to 0. Ok that is an oversimplification but I just want you to get the idea and this explains it sufficiently clear. Even in JavaScript if you had tried to add 1 to the letter 'a' instead of '0' the math would be wrong but the result would still be '1a' so the operation would complete. There are cases though where the arithmetic just would not make sense and you would get an undefined result anyway but before you get to that, you may be surprised how well JavaScript can calculate the square root of a cucumber!

So, if like me, you weren't brought up in JavaScript but in C++ or other languages that are strongly typed and would consider the above absolute sacrilege, then you need Typescript. Conversely, if you could not give two flips about this then you do not need TS at all. In any case, TS is optional.

So, what exactly does TS do? Well it does many things but here are the key ones:

- It converts JavaScript to JavaScript so whatever you do with TS will result in valid JavaScript - see more below;

- It allows you to structure your JavaScript code so that it looks like a strongly-typed language so you can define vars as strings or integers or anything else you may be more used to;

- It prevents you (via warnings) from calculating the square root of a cucumber because that just does not make any sense anyway though it can be useful at times;

- You can use classes, interfaces and modules and structure your code much more clearly;

- It is still all just JavaScript but it looks and feel nicer.

So, if you feel that you are getting lost in JavaScript's global vars and untyped variables, just use Typescript otherwise, pass. Here is the **TS reference site** with loads of tutorials and examples.

JavaScript

There are many great books and JavaScript (JS) guides. Here is one from the W3School. I recommend that you read that and also that you get a good reference book on JS so that you can learn at your own pace and use the book as a reference.

JS serves two purposes in applications development. First, it is your main coding language so any functionality your application provides (such as actually calculating the phases of the moon) will be done in JS. The second purpose is that JS can respond directly to events or actions taken in your program so, if you have a button that shows you the moon phase, clicking on that button and what happens next is handled by JS.

Both cases are really the same but I am trying to tell you that in addition to writing your own code and functions and calling them in JS, you will use JS also to handle your HTML page's need as well as JQuery's. Let's give you a few examples of both cases above...

JS to respond to JQuery or Page Events

One instance in which you will use JavaScript (JS) is to respond to events on a page. An event is an action that needs attention; it could be triggered by the press of a button or clicking on an image or simply typing on a field, among other things.

Events are handled the same by JS but if you are using JQuery there is a slightly different syntax used by JQuery which I will show you shortly.

One thing to consider is whether you insert the JS straight into INDEX.HTML (known as inline scripting) or whether to create a function in JS to handle the event. My recommendation is to completely avoid inline scripting because there are security issues associated with this. There is also the security tag (content security policy) that we discussed some time ago which usually prevents (you want it to) execution of inline scripts for safety reasons. So, you are best putting your scripts in a JS file and calling them from there.

Here is an example of an inline JS script...

```
<a href="#" onclick="alert(this)">You Clicked me!</a>
```

In the example above we have an <a> tag for a link and we added an **onclick** event handler so that when the user clicks on the link the code is executed; in this case, the code is a dialog box that says "You Clicked me!". This is an inline script in that it is embedded in the HTML. This is usually a bad idea for security reasons in case your HTML is compromised (people can replace your inline code with something else or make it do something else).

There is another way to execute inline JS by enclosing code inside of script tags like this:

```
<script>
document.getElementById("someelement").innerHTML = "Hello!";
</script>
```

Anything you put in between <script> tags is considered valid JS code that will be run as soon as the tag is encountered. This is also a bad idea as you are exposing code inside of the HTML that can be intercepted or changed but, this used to be the way to code a while back when things were not so unsafe.

To do these same things in a safer way you would create a script file (a file with the extension .js) and put your code there. In pure JS to do the above code inside of a script file you would declare a function so that when the element is clicked, this function would detect the click and respond like so:

```
someElement.onclick = function(){ code here };
```

This would be inside of a file so that when the "someElement" is clicked this function is called and your code ("code here") will run. JQuery does this slightly different although the purpose is the same. JQuery uses the symbol $ as a reference to JQuery itself and you can code a function to respond to a click event like this:

```
$('#someElement').on('click',function() {
     Your code here
});
```

Notice that the $ sign is just referencing JQuery to handle this event. The # sign means that what follows is an HTML element, it is as a matter of fact. very much equivalent to document.getElementById('someElement') so what follows the # sign is the id of an element in the HTML file which you are handling.

There are many events in that you can handle. The entirety of the web development model is referred to as the DOM (Document Object Model). I am referring you to **Mozilla** for a full description of the DOM. This is important because it shows you all available events and how to handle them. Where we wrote "click" above (an event) this can be replaced by many other events. You can see my developed example later to examine what other events and things I am handling.

JS to start creating your own code

So, you create JS code by creating files and putting JS in them. How does your HTML know what these files are so it can call them as needed? You insert a JS file reference inside of the HTML like so:

```html
<script type="text/javascript"
src="cordova.js"></script>

<!-- Platform Scripts -->
<script src="output/project.js"></script>

<!-- JS Algorithms -->
<script src="scripts/sMoon.js"></script>
<script src="scripts/sSaturn.js"></script>
<script src="scripts/sJupiter.js"></script>
```

Some things to comment on here:

- I usually put these at the end of the INDEX.HTML file before the closing of the HTML tag;

- I do that because if you put them in the beginning it may slow down showing the page;

- The **cordova.js** script is strictly necessary. It must be included and included **FIRST**;

- The project.js script is special - it is created by Typescript. If you use Typescript this is the only script you need unless you also used some files without JS (you can mix TS and JS) which I do in the last three scripts (sMoon, sSaturn and sJupiter) and that is why they are included also.

You can see my individual files in the image (left). So those are my script files and I included them in INDEX.HTML. Notice that **the order of these files matters**. For instance, if something in sSaturn calls sMoon (a function for instance) then sMoon needs to be included first otherwise sSaturn may not know what that function is.

So, what does the inside of a JS file look like - I referred you earlier to resources to learn JS but here is a peek inside of sMoon so you can see what it looks like:

```
var s_ProfileName = "Profile1";
var s_Latitude = 0;
var s_Longitude = 0;
var s_TimeZone = 0;
var s_DST = 0;
var s_NS = "N";
var s_EW = "W";


var CalendarData = [];


var ResetDate = true;
var MoonPhaseImage;
var NoonPreset = "00:00:00"; // use 12:00:00 for noon
or 00:00:00 to force midnight...


function FillGlobals() {
    try {
        let MainSettings;
        MainSettings                       = new
TideLock.MXSettings.cSettings();
```

```
MainSettings.LoadSettings();

    s_ProfileName = MainSettings.ProfileName;
    s_Latitude = MainSettings.Latitude;
    s_Longitude = MainSettings.Longitude;
    s_TimeZone = MainSettings.TimeZone;
    s_DST = (MainSettings.DST ? 1 : 0);
    s_NS = (MainSettings.North ? "N" : "S");
    s_EW = (MainSettings.East ? "E" : "W");
} catch (e) {


    }
}
```

I am mixing a little bit of JS and TS in there but you get the idea of what a code file looks like. This file defines a few variables at the top and then it proceeds to set up some global settings. You will do many more and many different things such as:

- Initializing the app;
- Loading the menu;
- Displaying pages;
- Handling clicks;
- Making Calculations;
- Many other things…

What you do of course is up to you and what your application is designed for. I am just sharing some of what I do to give you an idea.

Transpilation

I am going to revisit this topic in the next two sections but for now let me introduce you to the concept of Transpilation. Most people refer to Transpilation as a source-to-source compiler as opposed to a regular compiler which transforms source to binary or some other form.

Transpilation in our context refers to converting JS files to TS files or the other way around. Typically, when you write a TS file and you build your project, a Transpilation occurs that translates your source TS to source JS. In this manner, you could write all your code in TS and after build, it will be converted to JS which is what the browser and Cordova really understand. I will cover this in more detail later when I show you how to build your application using JSON files.

Targeting Mobile Platforms and Hardware

I told you a lot about what you need to know in terms of IDE's, Editors, Languages, Frameworks etc. However, I have not told you much about the devices themselves and the user experience. Remember that Cordova apps can run on the desktop but, in this section, I will talk to you about devices.

Design Guidelines

Designing your application is easy - making that design on different devices and platforms is hard and thus you will spend a lot of time deciding how to manage that complexity. Let me give you some examples of what I mean:

- After releasing your app, it seems to work fine on Android but not on Windows or IOS;
- You use a stylesheet that looks great on the emulator and it breaks down on the device;
- You created some nice fonts that look great when testing on the browser but look terrible on the device;
- You encounter unexpected exceptions when running the app on the device even though it runs great on the emulator;

- Your app looks beautiful until you turn the device sideways;
- Your app looks beautiful on your phone but terrible on a tablet.

The list can go on and on and on. Why do these things happen? Some things to take into consideration are:

- The emulator and the device are not the same. Emulators these days provide high fidelity but you need to test on a real device to ensure there are no problems (for instance, you could call a GPS function that is being simulated on the emulator but then on the device, GPS is turned off or behaves differently);

- Different devices and operating systems read your CSS differently - there is no real unified standard here despite the best efforts of the W3C. At the end of the day, a manufacturer of a browser may choose to differ from a standard and so things work on one browser but not on others. Regrettably, one great offender is Microsoft browsers. You may find that everything works well in Chrome and Firefox and Safari or Opera but not on IE or Edge. There used to be ways (and still there are) to insert HTML code to see which browser is running and adjust accordingly but quite frankly I find that most things work in all browsers very well but not on Microsoft browsers so I just do not target them;

- Devices are not the same. The size and capabilities of the device may cause you problems. Typical problems occur when you target a certain API (for instance, Android 7) but people run your app on Android 5. If you are using features exclusive to 7 you may run into problems on 5. One way around this is to specify in the config.xml which API's your app supports so a device with a lower API will communicate this to the user;

- OS' are not the same: Android, Windows Phone, IOS and others are not the same. The way they read and run your app may differ. The best way is to test on all devices if you can (there are cloud services that allow you to do this so you do not have to purchase all possible devices and many are free such as Intel XDK).

There may be many more reasons why these things happen so the list above is not all inclusive. The best thing you can do is to stick to design guidelines for each platform. You will find that most are common and shared and so, by following a few logical and standard principles you may avoid 99.9% of all possible problems.

What is my advice then?

- Adopt a UI framework and stick to it - this could be JQuery or Bootstrap. These are tested on all devices by their makers so you can be sure if you use them they are just going to work;

- Adopt a UX framework and stick to it. You may need to make some minor adjustments so they look better on different operating systems but in general they will work on all. Some people debate about having a **Google Material** look on an IOs device and there are valid points there; I am sure I am going to tick off marketing professionals and design individuals but I do not care if I run Material UI on IOS or Windows - it looks good anyway even if it was not originally meant for that device. As long as it represents your style and you like it, why not? I am not here to write according to IOS guidelines and be enslaved to them. I admit it would be weird to see a Windows App with flat design on an iPhone but well, it does not have to be that extreme;
- Consider and design for the User Experience. It does not matter if your app is great if nobody understands it or know how to use it. Sometimes you need to go great lengths to

make sure things are clear. I once had a person complain that my application was not a fitness app because it was called WeightLock even though it was pretty clear it was not a fitness app (heck this even happened to me with an astronomy app). Do not assume people know what is in your head or that they understand your app just because you do.

Usability Geek has some good articles on what to do and what not to do. Take a look at some of them.

Device Characteristics

This is going to be your biggest headache. It is not that you need to understand every single device in existence. All devices are different but they share some common principles and it is those principles you need to understand… This is a complex field; what I tell you here are starting guidelines - do read your device design guides for additional information.

Screens

What is the size of a device screen and what about its dimensions and density? If you make a font size 60 and you display that on a small screen that's going to be huge and out of bounds. So how do you know what to do?

The first answer to that question is - you should be using a UI design framework and relying on it to manage sizes. Do not specify absolute or arbitrary sizes or other design elements as they may only work on one device. Use metaphors for these such us "size medium" or "size small" instead of specifying dots or pixel sizes. Each device knows what you mean by small, medium or size text and they know which sizes to choose for the given device and those sizes will be different on other devices but they are cared for automatically.

Use responsive design. This type of design figures out screen dimensions and adapts all your elements to fit the width and the height in an elegant manner. Use this at all times.

You may need to create different pages for different generic device sizes. You can avoid this with responsive design or you may just need to provide a page view (layout) for a 4" device and another one for a 10" device because it just does not look right.

Images

Images are definitely a royal pain in the patella. If you try to put images on grids for instance, and your images are certain size, they may look good on a 6" screen and look minute on 12" screens or gigantic on 4" screens. What is the solution to this? There are two solutions…

1. Provide the same image in many different sizes for different resolutions and scaling. We will do that with application icons (I will show you later) and graphics but you can do this with all your images;

2. Provide one large image for all sizes and appeal to the display scaling functions that all devices have to shrink the image as needed. For instance, if you put images on grid using % for width and height, a large image will shrink to fit and it will look fine. A small image is no good as scaling up 2 or more times will show pixelation and it will look very poor.

Android has a fantastic resource **here** that explains everything you need to know about images, screens and designing for different sizes. Do take a look.

Device Capabilities

Capabilities are the abilities of a device to support certain functionality. For instance, can the device use a compass, does it have a temperature sensor, does it support orientation changes, etc.

Before you can implement certain features, such as GPS Navigation or mapping, you need to know if the device supports this. Cordova helps you query the device to see if these things are supported so, before you write a compass, ensure the device supports the functionality.

There is a Device plugin in Cordova that you can use to determine things such as:

- Cordova version number which can tell you which Cordova functions are available or not;
- Device model which can tell you what the device can do;
- Device platform if you don't really know you are running on Android or IOS;
- Device uuid - a unique identification number for the device which you can use in encryption or to ensure you are on a certain device;
- Device version - the version number of the device which reports useful things like Android 5.1 for instance;
- Device manufacturer - who made this device? Windows, Google, Apple, Samsung or anyone else;
- Device isVirtual - this reports yes if this is an emulator and no, otherwise;
- Device serial - the serial number of the device;

The information above can allow you to determine what a device can and cannot do even if just by cross referencing the manufacturer specifications so you know beforehand which devices will do what you want and which not. But there are other ways to determine if a device can perform certain functions. Here are two common ways:

- Perform the function and check for an error or a timeout. If any of those happen then the function cannot be performed;

- Ask the system if the function exist. Some systems like Android have functions that report if a FEATURE exists or not (such as, does this device have a camera or a rear camera)

You may also use **specialized cordova plugins** that do this for you. I linked you in the previous sentence to a plugin that can answer questions such as - is there Wi-Fi? Is there Bluetooth? Is there a Camera? And there are literally thousands of plugins you can leverage for this type of functionality.

Targeted Design - Merges

Ultimately, you may decide that you want to write the basic functionality of your application but then account for differences in platforms. You may choose to write common code once but then have three different UI's, images, or even scripts depending on what device you are on. If you decide to do this, which is a good decision to give your users the experience they desire (versus for instance, using a Windows Phone look on an iPhone). Cordova allows you to do this.

You can use the Cordova Device plugin to determine which OS you are on and then elect to display one UI or another, for instance, depending on the OS detected. This of course, requires you to design different sets of pages or styles that you can then select to display depending on the OS. You may accomplish this with Cordova Merges.

You may notice by opening and examining the directory tree that the "platforms" folder has different folders for each OS but also, if you look inside those folders, you will find copies of your WWW folder which contains your UI and code. You can make a "merges" folder in the root of your directory, just at the same level as the "platforms" folder is and then create subfolders for each platform (Android, etc.).

Inside the merges folder for, say, Android, you can create a CSS folder and put styles just for Android there. You can do this for any platform. When Cordova builds your project, it will check to see if these directories exist. If they do, it will copy files from there to the platform you are building for thus allowing you to have different CSS and even different scripts for each platform. Here is a good explanation of this process for your convenience.

Note that anything you do on your WWW folder applies to all platforms so, if you want common elements for all platforms do this on your WWW folder and add additional CSS or other types of files to the "merges" folders that contain different items for those platforms.

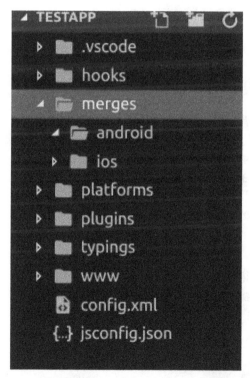

That sounds all a bit complicated so let's work through an example using a different CSS for Android and IOS. Open up the last project we created which is a simple Cordova application (TestApp on the "test" folder).

I just manually created the merges folder and also added an android folder and an IOS folder. They are empty.

Now, I am going to create a style in index.css which is in the WWW folder so it is common to every platform. It will contain a class for a label specifying the font size. I added the following line to index.css, right at the very top: **.aLabel { font-size: 24px; }**

Again, because the index.css file is in WWW (under CSS) it will be common to all platforms so, no matter what platform I use, the font size is going to be 24 points regardless.

Now I am going to add a CSS file to the android platform. I will call it Custom.css. Go to the merges/android folder, create a CSS folder and a file called Custom.CSS and add the following line to the file:

```
.aLabel { font-size: 60px; color:red;}
```

Don't forget to go to the top of Index.HTML now and add this new css like this:

```
<link rel="stylesheet" type="text/css"
href="css/Custom.css">
```

You can put this right below the index.css line if you will. Notice we are not specifying any merges location just css/Custom.css as if it were in fact inside of WWW even though it isn't. I did not add a Custom.css to the IOS folder but I could have and give it a different size and color if you wish. Normally, you would want to provide a Custom.css for all platforms, even if it is blank, because you are including a reference to this CSS file inside of index and you may get an error (file not found) for other platforms since they would not find this file.

Now, before you run your application, make one more change to INDEX.HTML so we can display a label of this class and you can see it. Put it somewhere like in the image below... Then run your application...

```
<body>
    <div class="app">
        <h1>Apache Cordova</h1>
        <div id="deviceready" class="blink">
            <p class="event listening">Connecting to Device</p>
            <p class="event received">Device is Ready</p>
        </div>
    </div>

    <p><label class="aLabel">Hi there</label></p>
    <script type="text/javascript" src="cordova.js"></script>
    <script type="text/javascript" src="js/index.js"></script>
```

This will run the app and display the text "Hi there" underneath the Cordova logo with size 60 and in red but in IOS, it will display this text per the style sheet index.css. So, there you go, two platforms, two stylesheets!

Life-cycle Management

Well, this is it! We have reached the point where I have no more background information to give you so, now that you know most of what you need to know, let's complete the picture for you and get hands on into developing an app. Before that, a few more concepts you have not learned yet and then we are ready…

Start Version Control

To prepare for the app we are going to write, let's initialize version control for this app. I explained this earlier but this will be a good recap.

We are going to create a folder for our new app, inside the same **"test"** folder we used before - this will just be another project. I intend to work on this app from different computers on my network so I am going to create a local repository, where I will do my development changes and a remote repository where I will push my changes so other computers can get them. You may place a remote repository in the cloud or you may use GitHub if you prefer for cloud repositories that can be access from any computer and anywhere (or just to share your work with others).

So, let's create a folder on my development machine which happens to be a Linux Mint 18.1 machine but we will also be able to work on this from Windows. I am creating a folder called **nTimer** in my "**test**" folder that I created earlier. I am doing this from within VSCODE so to recap:

- Right click on the "**test**" folder and open it with VSCODE
- Go to VSCODE's terminal and issue: **cordova create nTimer**;

Now, let's create a local git repository for **nTimer**

- In the VSCODE terminal type: **git init**. This creates a local repository.

Now, because I said I want this repository also on the network, I am going to go to my network drive and create an empty folder and also, I will call it **nTimer** but this time I am using this with a file manager…

- Use a file manager to go to your network location;
- Once there, create (manually) a folder and call it **nTimer**.

Get a command prompt or a terminal window open at that location or just open one and then navigate (Change Directory) to that location. Once there, issue the following command:

sudo git init --bare

In Windows, you do not need SUDO. This creates an empty (bare) repository that we can push to from our local repository.

However, we need to link these two together. To link them, open SmartGit. Perform the following steps:

1. Add your local repository to SmartGit by going to the menu and doing a **REPOSITORY >> ADD OR CREATE** and on the window that follows, browse to your local repository (**test/nTimer**) and add it. This will show you unstaged files since we just created the Cordova project;

2. Now link this repository to its remote counterpart by clicking on the SmartGit menu and choosing **REMOTE >> ADD** and in the window that appears, type the path to your remote repository (network/nTimer);

3. Confirm in the SmartGit output window that all is well. If so you should see something like the image on the top left of this page.

4. If all is well, let's create a gitIgnore file so that we do not have to add to our repository a bunch of intermediate and build files that we do not need. Go to your local repository, position yourself in the root and add a text file called gitignore (or .gitignore in Linux).

You can add whatever you need to this gitignore file which will case git not to add those files to the repository. A typical Cordova ignore file looks like this so, please feel free to just copy and paste this text into it...

```
# Android
platforms/android/assets/www
platforms/android/bin/
platforms/android/gen/
platforms/android/res/xml/config.xml

# iOS
```

```
platforms/ios/build/
platforms/ios/CordovaLib/build/
platforms/ios/www
platforms/ios/MyPace/config.xml
platforms/ios/.staging


# Emulator logs
platforms/ios/cordova/console.log
```

Save the file when you are done. If you are still looking at SmartGit (otherwise the next time you open it) you will notice that unwanted files are now gone and everything that remains to be staged is there. So, let's stage all these files right now - we can do this from VSCODE but since we are using SmartGit, we might as well do it from there. Go to the toolbar and choose **STAGE** - stage everything.

Once you have staged the files, let's commit them. Click **COMMIT** from the toolbar. Enter any comments you want for this commit and then, let's push it to the network repository by clicking **PUSH** from the toolbar.

Ok so now you have a local repository and a network one and they are in sync. From now on, every time you think appropriate (frequently please!) you go back to SmartGit and **stage** / **commit** / **push** so you can keep a version of all your changes in case you need it later. You can do this from VSCODE if you prefer as explained earlier. We are good now with version control - let's move on.

Add an android platform to your project. We are going to use Android for this sample app. Reopen the nTimer folder with VSCODE, go to the terminal and issue **cordova platform add android**. Ok, we are now ready to move on.

Automating Tasks with JSON

The time has come to show you how to introduce some automation here so you do not have to be issuing Cordova commands in the terminal all the time. Automation is accomplished in two ways:

1. Using JSON files;
2. Using the Extension bar in VSCODE

In fact, you will need to use both since they both do different things. Let's start with the VSCODE extension bar. To open it, press **CONTROL-SHIFT-P**. Notice how the bar opens up at the top;

Start typing the word "cordova" and you should see various options as in the image below. These are cordova tasks that come with the Cordova extension you installed a while ago. Instead of issuing BUILD or DEBUG commands you can access some predefined tasks from here. You may of course just keep using the terminal if you prefer that;

Try it now, press **CONTROL-SHIFT-P** and choose Cordova:Build. As you can see, this builds your project just like you did with the terminal. Do the same thing again and choose **Cordova Run** - see how your app now runs on the emulator just like when you typed RUN in the terminal.

Ok so feel free to use those built-in commands as you please. Now I am going to show you how to add your own to make other tasks easier.

JSON Files

I am going to quote this directly from Wikipedia to save me the trouble of saying something so complicated:

"In computing, JavaScript Object Notation or JSON (/ˈdʒeɪsən/ jay-sən),[1] is an open-standard format that uses human-readable text to transmit data objects consisting of attribute–value pairs and array data types (or any other serializable value). It is a very common data format used for asynchronous browser/server communication, including as a replacement for XML in some AJAX-style systems.[2]
JSON is a language-independent data format. It was derived from JavaScript, but as of 2017 many programming languages include code to generate and parse JSON-format data. The official Internet media type for JSON is application/json. JSON filenames use the extension .json."

Only JS could have come up with this eh? The definition is both brilliant and completely incomprehensible. Let me clear that for you...

JSON files are text files where you can specify a bunch of tasks that occur in sequence in order to achieve a goal. So, for instance, to build and sign your app, you can create a PACKAGE.JSON file and tell it with text, what commands need to be run to build and sign your app so you don't need to type them one at a time.

Ok, ok - I hear the cries! That is not all that JSON does - it can be a data interchange protocol and many other things but for us here in this guide, it is just a text file that tells VSCODE what to do. That is all we care about right now.

So, what types of JSON files do we need - we need no more and no less than the following JSON files (in order to automate our work):

- SETTINGS.JSON;
- LAUNCH.JSON;
- TASKS.JSON;
- BUILD.JSON;
- PACKAGE.JSON;
- TSCONFIG.JSON.

That is all that we need. Each of these files allows us to automate something so let me explain in order of priority what these files are and what they have inside. This explanation will cover what you need to know but no more so, I am not going to fill your mind with a load of JSON settings we do not care about but do be aware that there are many settings so you can look them up if you want to add more customization.

SETTINGS.JSON

This file controls VSCODE settings - I do not normally do anything with these files except to add a line to hide Typescript map files and redundant JS files so the only thing I need to do is add the following lines to the empty SETTINGS.JSON file:

```
{
"files.exclude":                                        {
    "**/*.js":      {      "when":      "$(basename).ts"},
    "**/*.map":                                       true
  }
}
```

TSCONFIG.JSON

This file is critical to the workings of Typescript and it must exist in the root of your project folder (unless you plan not to use TS). Feel free to paste this into it:

```
{
    "compilerOptions":                              {
        "noImplicitAny":                        false,
        "noEmitOnError":                         true,
        "removeComments":                        true,
        "sourceMap":                             true,
        "inlineSources":                         true,
        "module":                               "amd",
        "out":              "www/output/project.js",
        "target":                               "es5"
    },
    "exclude":                                      [
        "platforms",
        "node_modules",
        "bower_components",
        "plugins",
        "merges",
        "res",
        "bin",
        "bld"]
}
```

The most important things you need to know about this file is this:

"Out": this is the location of the output file of the Transpilation process. Recall that Transpilation takes all your TS files and all your JS files and it converts them into a single JS file that you include in your INDEX.HTML - this is the location where that file will be put so you can include it in your project. This is generated during the BUILD process (explained below).

"Target": this is the version of the JavaScript standard you want to use. JS changes over the years and as it changes, it offers newer and improved functionality and it also obsoletes or "deprecates" older functionality. The current standard for JS is ES6 but a lot of people use ES5. I use ES6 as it is the latest one and it offers more features.

"Exclude": these are files that we do not want to bother with during build and transpilation because they are not needed by the compiler so they can be freely ignored. They need to be ignored also because you may have some JS files in there you don't want to include in the project so you must specify folders you want to ignore (or none if not bothered). Including not needed folders speeds up the build as the compiler is not looking for files in them and some folders like "platforms" can be very huge.

TASKS.JSON

When you build your application (which can be accomplished by pressing CONTROL-SHIFT-B) a task is needed to automate the build. This file contains instructions to transpile. You will recall that we could run our cordova app without this file. This is because we were not using any TS in our sample TestApp. But if you include TS or any other language that needs an external tool to compile it, you need one or more TASKS.JSON files to tell VSCODE where the compiler is so it can be invoked during the build process. The TS compiler is called TSC.

Here is a perfectly good and usable (paste it) TASKS.JSON file:

```
{
    "version":                          "0.1.0",
    "command":                          "tsc",
    "isShellCommand":                   true,
    "args":             ["-p",          "."],
    "showOutput":                       "silent",
    "problemMatcher":                   "$tsc"
}
```

LAUNCH.JSON

This file contains information on how to run and debug your application. You may add more than one way to run and debug your app by specifying individual configuration (in between curly brackets) for instance for a device, for a browser, for the emulator, etc. Here is an example file:

```
{
    "version":                              "0.2.0",
    "configurations":                            [
        {
            "name":    "Run    Android    on   device",
            "type":                        "cordova",
            "request":                      "launch",
            "platform":                    "android",
            "target":                       "device",
            "port":                            9222,
            "sourceMaps":                      true,
            "cwd":                "${workspaceRoot}",
            "ionicLiveReload":                false
        },
        {
            "name":    "Run    iOS    on    device",
            "type":                        "cordova",
            "request":                      "launch",
            "platform":                        "ios",
            "target":                       "device",
            "port":                            9220,
            "sourceMaps":                      true,
            "cwd":                "${workspaceRoot}",
            "ionicLiveReload":                false
        },
        {
            "name":  "Attach  to  running  android  on
device",
            "type":                        "cordova",
            "request":                      "attach",
            "platform":                    "android",
```

```
            "target":                        "device",
            "port":                          9222,
            "sourceMaps":                    true,
            "cwd":                 "${workspaceRoot}"
    },
    {

            "name": "Attach to running iOS on device",
            "type":                          "cordova",
            "request":                       "attach",
            "platform":                      "ios",
            "target":                        "device",
            "port":                          9220,
            "sourceMaps":                    true,
            "cwd":                 "${workspaceRoot}"
    },
    {

            "name":   "Run   Android   on   emulator",
            "type":                          "cordova",
            "request":                       "launch",
            "platform":                      "android",
            "target":                        "emulator",
            "port":                          9222,
            "sourceMaps":                    true,
            "cwd":                 "${workspaceRoot}",
            "ionicLiveReload":               false
    },
    {

            "name":   "Run   iOS   on   simulator",
            "type":                          "cordova",
            "request":                       "launch",
            "platform":                      "ios",
            "target":                        "emulator",
            "port":                          9220,
            "sourceMaps":                    true,
            "cwd":                 "${workspaceRoot}",
            "ionicLiveReload":               false
    },
    {

            "name":   "Attach   to   running   android   on
```

```
emulator",
        "type":                              "cordova",
        "request":                            "attach",
        "platform":                          "android",
        "target":                           "emulator",
        "port":                                  9222,
        "sourceMaps":                            true,
        "cwd":                        "${workspaceRoot}"
    },
    {
        "name":  "Attach  to  running  iOS  on
simulator",
        "type":                              "cordova",
        "request":                            "attach",
        "platform":                              "ios",
        "target":                           "emulator",
        "port":                                  9220,
        "sourceMaps":                            true,
        "cwd":                        "${workspaceRoot}"
    },
    {
        "name":  "Serve  to  the  browser  (ionic
serve)",
        "type":                              "cordova",
        "request":                            "launch",
        "platform":                            "serve",
        "cwd":                       "${workspaceRoot}",
        "devServerAddress":              "localhost",
        "sourceMaps":                            true,
        "ionicLiveReload":                       true
    },
    {
        "name": "Simulate Android in browser",
        "type":                              "cordova",
        "request":                            "launch",
        "platform":                          "android",
        "target":                             "chrome",
        "simulatePort":                          8000,
        "livereload":                            true,
```

```
        "sourceMaps":                        true,
        "cwd":                  "${workspaceRoot}"
    },
    {

        "name":    "Simulate    iOS    in    browser",
        "type":                         "cordova",
        "request":                       "launch",
        "platform":                         "ios",
        "target":                        "chrome",
        "simulatePort":                      8000,
        "livereload":                        true,
        "sourceMaps":                        true,
        "cwd":                  "${workspaceRoot}"
    }
  ]
}
```

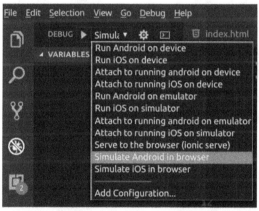

This file has configurations for IOS, Android, Devices, Emulators, Browsers, etc. Paste this and you are covered.

If you are wondering how to select a configuration to run, VSCODE allows you to this from the configuration dropdown on the debug section (see image).

As you can see, everything in the JSON file is in there.

BUILD.JSON

This file specifies how to build your application. Since you are using Cordova you do not really need this file except sometimes I use it to specify my KeyStore to sign the app (this is optional but you might use it for it.) In those cases, I just specify the location of the KeyStore (discussed in later sections) like so:

```
{"android": {
        "release": { keystore": "wherever your store
is",
        "storePassword": "password",
            "alias": "alias", password" : "password"
}}
```

I do not normally code the keystore like that or I let all entries blank. This causes the cordova build process to ask me for my passwords so I do not have to list them here.

PACKAGE.JSON

This file tells your project how to package the app. Since you are using Cordova and it already knows how to pack and sign the app, you do not really need it but when you deploy the app to the desktop you will need it so we will revisit this file later when we get to Electron and creating desktop apps. For now, you can just create a simple file and type this into it:

```
{
    "name":                              "TideLock",
    "version":                            "2.0.8",
    "private":                              true,
    "dependencies":                            {
    }
}
```

Application Manifest

Let's talk about the **application manifest** for Android. One good thing about Cordova's CONFIG.XML file is that it is essentially the manifest. A manifest is needed by the stores to examine what your application is about, what permissions it requires, how it is structured, what images, icons, splashes you want to use, who you are, etc. Android apps built with Android Studio have a manifest.xml file that you must fill as you go. Cordova has CONFIG.XML and it literally builds an Android Manifest from the information in this file plus other internal data.

So, what you really need to understand is what to put in CONFIG.XML and then if you wish, after building your app you can go into the platform output folders and take a look at the manifests that Cordova created from this.

So, your manifest is CONFIG.XML - it is time to complete your training on this file. Let's list one from my TideLock app here for a complete example:

```xml
<?xml version="1.0" encoding="utf-8"?>
<widget xmlns:cdv="http://cordova.apache.org/ns/1.0"
xmlns:vs="http://schemas.microsoft.com/appx/2014/htmlapp
s" id="com.Madvox.TideLock" version="2.0.8"
xmlns="http://www.w3.org/ns/widgets" defaultlocale="en-
US" android-versionCode="3" windows-
packageVersion="2.0.8.0">
 <name>TideLock</name>
 <description>Detailed ephemeris of the moon and solar
system objects</description>
 <author href="http://www.madvox.com"
email="admin@madvox.com">Madvox LLC</author>
 <vs:template-name>BlankTS</vs:template-name>
 <vs:toolsetVersion>6.3.1</vs:toolsetVersion>
 <engine name="android" spec="5.2.1" />
 <engine name="windows" spec="4.4.2" />
 <content src="index.html" />
 <plugin name="cordova-plugin-whitelist" spec="1.2.2" />
 <access origin="*" />
 <allow-intent href="http://forecast.weather.gov" />
 <allow-navigation href="http://forecast.weather.gov" />
 <preference name="SplashScreen" value="screen" />
 <preference name="FadeSplashScreen" value="false" />
 <preference name="windows-target-version" value="10.0"
```

```
/>
 <!-- Support for Cordova 5.0.0 plugin system -->
 <platform name="android">
   <allow-intent href="market:*" />
 </platform>
 <platform name="android">
   <icon src="logos/icons/android/icon-36-ldpi.png"
density="ldpi" />
   <icon src="logos/icons/android/icon-48-mdpi.png"
density="mdpi" />
   <icon src="logos/icons/android/icon-72-hdpi.png"
density="hdpi" />
   <icon src="logos/icons/android/icon-96-xhdpi.png"
density="xhdpi" />
 </platform>
 <platform name="windows">
   <icon
src="logos/icons/windows/Square150x150Logo.scale-
100.png" width="150" height="150" />
   <icon
src="logos/icons/windows/Square150x150Logo.scale-
240.png" width="360" height="360" />
   <icon src="logos/icons/windows/Square30x30Logo.scale-
100.png" width="30" height="30" />
   <icon
src="logos/icons/windows/Square310x310Logo.scale-
100.png" width="310" height="310" />
   <icon src="logos/icons/windows/Square44x44Logo.scale-
100.png" width="44" height="44" />
   <icon src="logos/icons/windows/Square44x44Logo.scale-
240.png" width="106" height="106" />
   <icon src="logos/icons/windows/Square70x70Logo.scale-
100.png" width="70" height="70" />
   <icon src="logos/icons/windows/Square71x71Logo.scale-
100.png" width="71" height="71" />
   <icon src="logos/icons/windows/Square71x71Logo.scale-
240.png" width="170" height="170" />
   <icon src="logos/icons/windows/StoreLogo.scale-
100.png" width="50" height="50" />
   <icon src="logos/icons/windows/StoreLogo.scale-
240.png" width="120" height="120" />
   <icon src="logos/icons/windows/Wide310x150Logo.scale-
100.png" width="310" height="150" />
```

```xml
    <icon src="logos/icons/windows/Wide310x150Logo.scale-
240.png" width="744" height="360" />
  </platform>
  <platform name="android">
    <splash src="logos/screens/android/screen-hdpi-
landscape.png" density="land-hdpi" />
    <splash src="logos/screens/android/screen-ldpi-
landscape.png" density="land-ldpi" />
    <splash src="logos/screens/android/screen-mdpi-
landscape.png" density="land-mdpi" />
    <splash src="logos/screens/android/screen-xhdpi-
landscape.png" density="land-xhdpi" />
    <splash src="logos/screens/android/screen-hdpi-
portrait.png" density="port-hdpi" />
    <splash src="logos/screens/android/screen-ldpi-
portrait.png" density="port-ldpi" />
    <splash src="logos/screens/android/screen-mdpi-
portrait.png" density="port-mdpi" />
    <splash src="logos/screens/android/screen-xhdpi-
portrait.png" density="port-xhdpi" />
  </platform>
  <platform name="windows">
    <splash
src="logos/screens/windows/SplashScreen.scale-100.png"
width="620" height="300" />
    <splash
src="logos/screens/windows/SplashScreen.scale-240.png"
width="1152" height="1920" />
    <splash
src="logos/screens/windows/SplashScreenPhone.scale-
240.png" width="1152" height="1920" />
  </platform>
  <plugin name="cordova-plugin-device" spec="~1.1.5" />
  <plugin name="cordova-plugin-vibration" spec="~2.1.4"
/>
  <plugin name="cordova-plugin-splashscreen"
spec="~4.0.2" />
  <plugin name="cordova-plugin-inappbrowser"
spec="~1.7.0" />
  <preference name="android-minSdkVersion" value="15" />
  <preference name="android-targetSdkVersion" value="23"
/>
  <preference name="ShowTitle" value="True" />
```

```
 <preference name="WindowsStoreDisplayName"
value="TideLock" />
 <vs:platformSpecificValues>
   <vs:platformSpecificWidget platformName="windows"
id="xxxxxMadvox.TideLock" version="2.0.8.0" />
 </vs:platformSpecificValues>
 <preference name="WindowsStoreDisplayName"
value="TideLock" />
 <preference name="KeepRunning" value="true" />
 <preference name="ShowTitle" value="True" />
 <preference name="InAppBrowserStorageEnabled"
value="True" />
 <preference name="SuppressesIncrementalRendering"
value="True" />
 <plugin name="cordova-plugin-splashscreen"
version="3.1.0" />
 <preference name="WindowsStoreIdentityName"
value="xxxxxMadvox.TideLock" />
 <preference name="WindowsStorePublisherName"
value="you" />
</widget>
```

This is very important so let's dissect this file. I bolded some self-explanatory items in the file so just know that the bolded statements represent basic information such as your name, your app name, your store name for windows, your email and easy stuff like that. If you do not know how to handle the store names I will cover that in next section.

Other critical parts of the file:

```
<plugin name="cordova-plugin-whitelist" spec="1.2.2"
/>
 <access                    origin="*"                    />
 <allow-intent href="http://forecast.weather.gov" />
 <allow-navigation
href="http://forecast.weather.gov"                    />
```

This is a security section. The Access Origin and the intent and navigation statements specify which servers your app is allowed to talk to. If you specify none, no communications via internet will be allowed. In my case, I need weather info so I specify the weather serves I need to talk to, in this case the North Oceanic Atmospheric Administration forecast servers.

```
<plugin name="cordova-plugin-device" spec="~1.1.5" />
<plugin name="cordova-plugin-vibration" spec="~2.1.4" />
<plugin name="cordova-plugin-splashscreen" spec="~4.0.2" />
<plugin name="cordova-plugin-inappbrowser" spec="~1.7.0" />
<plugin name="cordova-plugin-splashscreen" version="3.1.0" />
```

Plugins are added automatically by Cordova so you do not need to worry but I am showing you what plugin listing looks like.

For android, your minimum supported API and desired API are needed:

```
<preference name="android-minSdkVersion" value="15" />
<preference name="android-targetSdkVersion" value="23" />
```

These preferences are entirely your choice. If you choose to support SDK 26 which the latest version of Android that is ok. But do be aware of what the minimum SDK is because your app will not run on devices below this number. This of course is also up to you but understand that the minimum SDK does establish a minimal requirement for your app to run.

The rest of the file is full of statements like this:

```
<platform name="android">
    <icon  src="logos/icons/android/icon-36-ldpi.png"
density="ldpi" />
    <icon  src="logos/icons/android/icon-48-mdpi.png"
density="mdpi" />
    <icon  src="logos/icons/android/icon-72-hdpi.png"
density="hdpi" />
    <icon src="logos/icons/android/icon-96-xhdpi.png"
density="xhdpi" />
</platform>
```

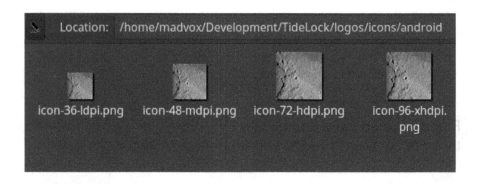

These statements specify the location of your asset (image) files needed for the store. This includes icons and screenshots. You must include them in every required resolution. My example CONFIG.XML include all needed assets so if you create your images and replace the text above you will have everything needed.

Prepare, Building, Running and Testing

Let's move into how to build, run and test an app. You already know how to build an app but what exactly does building an app mean?

The build process has a specific workflow but summarizing, BUILD will examine your code for errors, examine all dependencies you need to run your app, compile the application into a package that can be run and leave it in a state where you can then actually run or debug the app. Let's go into details…

Preparation

Cordova has a preparation phase before BUILD that moves image files to the destination platform folders, revises merges and makes sure the app can be built. While you can go ahead and build the app without preparation, issuing a PREPARE command on its own can be useful to see if something is not right prior to building.

Building

The build process (which will issue an implicit PREPARE command anyway) then assembles all these assets and compiles them into an executable file or a package (APK for instance) that you can then run and debug.

Running & Debugging

You can run the application in debug or release mode. By default, applications are set to run in debug mode. You must turn debug mode off when you are ready to build a release version of your app. When building an app with Cordova you can also specify if you want to build a debug version or a release version (**cordova build release** will build a signed version of your app and **cordova build** assumes you want a debug version).

Testing

You may test your app by adding debug breakpoints and have the run process pause as you need to examine variables (variable watch). You may also test in the Chrome browser and use the developer functions and the logging console to monitor your application. Chrome has many facilities for debugging as you can see in the image below…

Putting it all together

Let's put it all together in an example session. Let's add a bit more substance to our nTimer app and build it, run it, debug it and test it.

Run and Test the app

We are not yet writing a large app - we will do that shortly and we will have a chance to see many more details about the application development process. For now, I want to make sure you understand the process so far so let us return to our **nTimer** app, from the "**test**" folder and figure out how to run and debug the app. This is an iterative part of the development process where you will make changes to your app and then run it and debug it to make sure all is good. Once you are satisfied your application is complete and working you can build a final release and signed version of it.

We will stay with Android for this example but remember that Cordova can target many other platforms so if you wish to experiment with Windows or IOS or others, nothing much changes here unless you are providing specific platform code through "merges", as explained earlier.

Release and Debug Configurations

When are developing an application, you want to be in debug mode so that you can insert breakpoints and examine your code as it runs. In debug mode, the system generates debug symbols and the debugger responds to granular control on how the application is executing so that you can pause it and look for errors and exceptions or understand why certain things are not working.

When your application is complete and you are comfortable that everything is working fine, you will build your application in release mode. This removes symbols and extra files needed for debugging that are not needed for your final production version of the app and thus it does not unnecessarily clutter it with extra files.

A release application also needs to be signed before it can be put in a store. Later, I will show you how you can run unsigned applications for testing purposes but ultimately, you need to sign your app if you are planning to put it on a store.

As with debug mode, when you build your release application you need to test it thoroughly one more time. Because changes are made to the app executable depending on whether it is a debug executable or a release one, you need to ensure your release build is still working as expected.

So how does running and debugging the app work? You already know that a **cordova run** command runs the app but how do you debug it? For this we have two options. Normally, you would have one option which is to use the built-in debugger in VSCODE or any other IDE or tool but because our app is a web app, it can be emulated on a browser and from Chrome, for instance, you can use the browser's built-in debugging tools as well if that is something you already know or enjoy. Let's take a look at both cases but first, let's explain how different debugging options are chosen.

Debug Options

Remember when we talked about LAUNCH.JSON?

This file is responsible for populating a drop down in VSCODE that lets you choose your debug preferences. In our LAUNCH.JASON we had entries such as this (examine the whole file quickly so you can see the other options):

```
{
        "name": "Run Android on emulator",
        "type": "cordova",
        "request": "launch",
        "platform": "android",
        "target": "emulator",
        "port": 9222,
        "sourceMaps": true,
        "cwd": "${workspaceRoot}",
        "ionicLiveReload": false
}
```

This is an entry that provides the option to run on the android emulator. Other entries allow you to run on the browser or the device, etc. Where is this option selectable? Look at the image above: The icon with the crossed bug is the debugger menu - pressing that button is how we got to this screen. Then, on the top menu there is a drop down next to DEBUG which is where the options in LAUNCH.JSON are displayed. This is how you can select one of the available options.

Once you have selected an option you like, press the green "play" button next to debug to start. However, because you have not inserted any breakpoints, the application runs without stopping anywhere.

Breakpoints

Breakpoints are lines of code where you can stop the execution of your application (rather pause, not stop) in order to take a look at what is going on. After pausing, you can resume execution to look at other things.

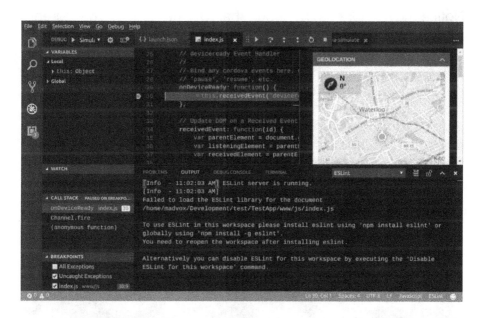

To insert a breakpoint all you need to do is left-click on your code just to the left of any line number. For instance, since we do not have much code in this example application, I went to INDEX.JS inside the JS folder and put a breakpoint on the DeviceReady function - just for a test. See the image showing this, put a breakpoint just where I put it and run your app now and watch how it does stop right on that line…

Notice that when the app stops, as you can see in the figure above, you can watch local and global variables or insert your own to check the state of things. You may insert your own under "Watch".

▲ WATCH

▲ this: Object {initialize...
  ▶ initialize: function (...

Aside from watches and variable inspections, you can see where your code is paused at and run the program one line at a time back and forth continuing to ensure all is well.

Notice how there is a debug bar at the top of the screen, reproduced here so that you can recognize it. It contains a number of navigation buttons for the debugger. The first button, the green play arrow, will simply continue execution without pausing any more unless it hits another breakpoint. The down arrow allows you to step inside of a function call (so it will pause inside of the next function you are calling). The rounded arrow steps over your current line and proceeds to the next one. And finally, the up arrow is used to execute a function and step out of it back to the caller. The green refresh arrow will stop all actions and restart the debugger from the beginning and finally, the red square stops the debugger. Press the some of these now and get a feel for what they do. When done, press the red square to exit the debugger.

The other way to debug, as mentioned earlier, is to not debug using VSCODE but simply run your application in a browser (like Chrome) and press F12 for the developer tools on the browser. Chrome has a number of debugging tools as well and they do much of the same as VSCODE does except Chrome calls your attention to issues on StyleSheets and HTML as well. In a way, you are better off using Chrome if you are having issues with your styles or HTML and use VSCode for JavaScript. Either way is a good way to debug so much is down to preference.

Testing your App

So now you know how to run and debug your application. In larger IDE's, testing can be very in-depth indeed. You can create testing scripts or functions that run, in many cases automatically, as your program runs, informing you of the results of tests and where there might be problems. There are entire testing frameworks designed to help you alpha test, beta test, create testing projects, automation scripts etc. These are all fantastic and I will let you explore some of those (included in the appendix) at your own pace but... for the purposes of our guide which is introductory or intermediate, we will not get overly complicated with these things.

For our guide, we are going to go mostly manual on testing but this is a good thing as you can learn the ropes first and then pursue deeper means if you wish. But we are going to test the old fashion way. I recommend that you create a text file in the root of your project and call it "defects.txt" or "tests.txt" so you can annotate and keep track of problems as you test. You may put this file in SmartGit too to keep track of all changed you are making. Some people ultimately use the contents of a file such as this to create a version history or a log of all the changes that were made to the app - a combination of new or changed features you added and the results of testing or bug fixing. It is not uncommon for application developers to publish sections of this document as Patch Notes or Bug Fixes (sometimes as a Readme.ME file) or just the entire history of the app.

I have simple advice for you so that we do not get too complex right now. I usually create three sections in this file:

#New Features since Version xx
#Bug Fixes and problems solved since Version xx
#Other (for instance, maintenance made or historical version changes, etc.)

You may of course add more or less sections as you wish. I do keep this file under version control and many times, whatever I put in this file is used as the "commit" message for GIT. At regular intervals, when I feel I made significant changes, I may change version numbers (more on this below) and add tags to GIT to indicate this is a new version of the app. I will show you some of this below. To give you an idea, here is a briefly worked out TEST.TXT file...

```
#Application History
This is TideLock 2.0.8 - Release in production

#Added since 2.0.5
    • New Moon Calendar View
    • Added more details to phase display, including
      Rising and Setting Times

# Added since 2.0.1
    • Planetary Ephemeris
    • Lunar Eclipses

#....


# Version 1
    • Created the application for the first time...
```

You can go on like this as much as you want and add bug fixes and defects or any other information you need.

Versions and Builds Numbers

Versioning your application does not need to be difficult but you do need some kind of versioning because the app stores want to know which version of the app you are using so they can notify users of updates or changes as needed. You should never upload a changed application with the same version number as a prior upload as this may confuse everyone since you changed the app but we cannot tell. Luckily, most if not all stores will stop you right there and request a new version number.

So, what is a version number? It is a log that keeps track of how many times you have changed the app. The version number is up to you so you may see people with very simple version numbers, such as 1, 2, 3 etc.... (every change they make they up the number by one) or the more common 1.0, 1.1. 1.2, 2.0 etc.... which is more granular. You may also see things like this: 3.45.12005.4097 - larger companies, larger codebases and people who build daily or hourly (perhaps using automation) do keep track of many more things in the version number. For instance, the number above may represent version 3, revision 45, 12005 builds since the beginning, 4097 builds this revision or something like that.

There is really no need to get complicated and so I recommend you use a system such as x.y.z with z being optional. X would be your main version number (1, 2, 3 etc....) and Y will be your revision number (supposed you released version 1.0 but then found a bug and made a change so this would now be 1.1 but not 2 since you did not add anything new). Additionally, you may use Z for your build number. A lot of people care about build numbers and many do not so it is up to you. A build number records how many times you built your app (it may represent other things to other people but primarily that is what it does). So, 1.0.300 would mean version 1, no revisions, took 300 builds to get to it.

For me personally, I do not care about build numbers. What does it matter how many times I compiled the app? Perhaps I compile every time I make a change or perhaps I compile at the end of the day or every week. The number is fairly meaningless to me. But to larger enterprises it may be very meaningful as you may roll back by build number if something is wrong, and not by version number, among other possibilities.

So, start by sticking to a simple code like this, and you will be fine:

- Use the schema x.y.z
- Use x for your main version number (e.g. 1.0.0 or 2.0.0);
- Use y for revisions (e.g. 1.1.0 or 2.5.0);
- Optionally, use Z for build numbers or any other number meaningful to you.

A main version number increments by one if you added features or perhaps if the features you added are significant from the prior version. A revision number is used if you add features but they are not huge differences or if you make any changes as a result of bugs or problems. And Z can be used sometimes for a date not just a build number so, you could say your program version is 2.8.20170504 (the last digits being May 4th, 2017).

Whatever you do, recall that this number needs to be plugged into Config.XML as we showed you in earlier sections.

Emulation

Emulation refers to the ability to run your app not on a device. Further below I am going to show you how to run your test application on a device but since running the app on the device is more involved than the emulator, I will talk about emulation - which is what you will use most of the time - until you are ready to test on a device.

You saw in the earlier section that LAUNCH.JSON is used to specify where the application will run. You may run it on devices or on emulators and the Chrome browser does count as an emulator (it adds features to test your app). So, from the drop down next to the debugger run command that we spoke earlier, you can see that you can run the application as:

1. On a device
2. Attach to a running emulator (Android or other)
3. On an emulator
4. On a browser

You could always add more options of course but the advantage of the browser and the emulators is that they allow you to start-and-run your application on the spot without having to load up a device. Ultimately, you want to test your app on a device but before you are done writing it, it is far more convenient to use an emulator.

So, what emulator is better Chrome or a regular device emulator. My advice is to always use a device emulator because this uses a version of the OS (e.g. Android) that closely mimics the real device. Having said that, I also like debugging in Chrome because it has facilities to see if there is anything at all wrong with your stylesheets or your HTML and the device emulator does not look at these much. So perhaps the best advice is a combination of both - if you are debugging code, strictly, use the device emulator. If you are debugging your UI, you may be better off with Chrome.

Device Emulation

For device emulation you may use Android, Windows, IOS or any other device if you set additional ones up. The emulator will do a good job of closely resembling the device except, some functions may not be available (e.g. it may not have a compass or it may not be able to connect to the Internet depending on your set up).

Windows (via the Windows 10 SDK) provides a series of emulators you can use. Android (via the Android SDK) does the same and although I do not have much experience in IOS, I am sure the situation is the same. You may run the emulator when your program starts (e.g. **Run Android on Emulator**) or you may open up an emulator, keep it open, then attach to it (e.g. **Attach to running Android on Emulator**). I prefer to run the emulator when my app is started because I am on a lower spec dev machine (for convenience reasons) and so keeping the emulator running using up 2 gigs of RAM all the time is not particularly effective for me but, if you have the memory, please feel free to keep it going to save initialization time.

Unless you opened up an emulator and attach to it, the application will open one for you when you press **RUN**. The emulator that will pop up will be whatever default emulator you have set up in the SDK. So, for instance, for Android, if a Nexus 7 emulator pops up that is because you have it set as default or, in the absence of defaults, it is the first one it finds. If you want instead to run on a Nexus 4 or something else, you may launch it and attach or change your defaults in the AVD manager.

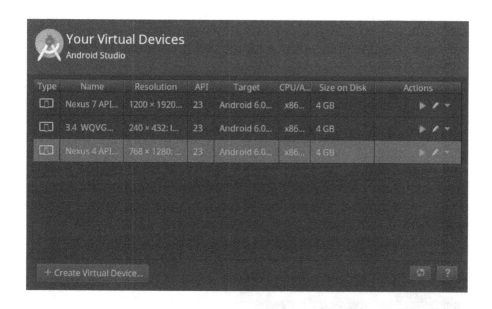

Go ahead and run your application again and do choose to run it on the Android Emulator and play around with it.

For my own purposes, I opened up a Nexus 4 emulator so that you can see on this figure at the left, that it looks the same as an original device running this version of Android.

It is important that you know that using the Android AVD or the windows SDK you can configure any number of device emulators. This is important as you can test your application multiple times on difference emulated devices.

I have sometimes noticed that an application that works fine on a device, does not on another and it is typically because of some settings you've declared (or not declared) such as what is the minimum SDK version required or the target version. This may happen on any platform, including desktops so ensure that your application is designed to run on the emulator before you test. Be sure to test different form factors as well (such as a tablet or a small phone) so that you can see how your application behaves - perhaps you designed it for a tablet and it does not fit on a small phone.

Browser Emulation

As I mentioned earlier the browser can be a great aid for your UI but it can also debug your code. It can be very convenient to run on Chrome since it is quite fast at loading your application and as indicated, it can debug your scripts not just your UI. Here is a screenshot of Chrome in action on my TideLock application:

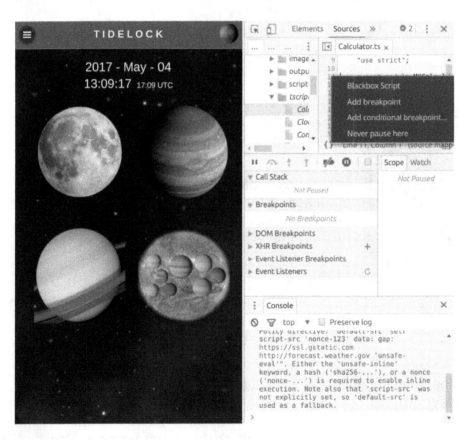

You can see the app side-by-side with the debugger - some warnings in my HTML and on top right, I opened up my calculator script and I can add breakpoints and debug as needed. This is a great option overall as it debugs any device (including desktops) without having to launch a specialized emulator.

Device Connectivity

A third form of running your application is not to emulate it at all. You may plug your device via a USB cable to your development computer and access the device via a specific port. This is specified in LAUNCH.JSON so feel free to plug a device in and test the app - this will work fine with the app being debugged also being deployed to your real device. A lot of people test and debug this way and this is a great way to debug especially if you are using functions that are not operative on the emulators (such as GPS or location tracking, etc.)

The other way to run your application on the device is to copy the APK over to it and run it from there. This of course is disconnected from the debugger so you will be running your app on a real device but you cannot debug it - it is more for checking that things are appearing in the right places and that the overall look and feel as well as performance of the app are ok.

If you want to deploy your signed or unsigned app to your device for this purpose, you will need to first go to the device settings and usually under security (in the case of Android) there is an option to allow for third party sources or apps to be installed. Check this and click OK on the warning that this may be harmful (it can be harmful indeed but since it is you and your app doing this, you are fine). **Later, when you install the app, come back to this setting and turn it off to be safe.**

Once you have done that, make sure you copy your APK from the platform build directories on your development machine (typically, in Android, your APK will be located in /platforms/android/build/outputs/apk and the file will be named android-debug.apk if it is unsigned or android-release.ask if it is. Both will run fine on your device so, copy the file to perhaps a network location and then open a file manager on the device. Locate the file and run it - this will cause the device to install your application just as if you had downloaded it from a store. You may now run your app and inspect it as needed.

Submitting and Releasing the Application

Signing an Application

You will need to sign your application before you can put it in a store. Signing your application is a two-step process. The first thing you need is a Keystore of your own that you can use in the future to sign all your applications. Once you have the store you can then use it successively to sign applications by making a reference to the Key store in BUILD.JSON.

So, first things first, you need to create a Keystore, define your keys and passwords and save the file securely somewhere that your application can find. When setting up the keystore remember that this contains your digital signature so it is very important that you assign strong passwords to your keystore - you do not want this to be easily accessed nor do you want to share your keys with anyone. This is why I do not enter a password in BUILD.JSON - you can simply enter your keystore name and you will be asked for the password at build time.

There are several ways to create a store - the easiest ways probably involve opening up Visual Studio or Android Studio and creating the store once (you can then reuse it as needed). But I can understand you would not want to install those massive tools just to make a store. So here is a command you can use from the VSCODE terminal. When you are done, move the keystore to a safe location:

```
keytool -genkey -v -keystore MyKeys.keystore -alias
MyKeysAlias -keyalg RSA -keysize 2048 -validity 10000
```

Note that the 10000 number above is the duration of the key in days (10,000 in this case. You can enter any number you want here. 10k days will give you a good 27.4 years of validity anyway!

When you issue this command, the tool will ask you for your name, country, passwords for the keystore, etc. Just answer as you would want things to be and you will be fine. Note that the name of the store is MyKeys.keystore and the alias name is MyKeysAlias but you can of course use any names you want.

When this is done, your store and its private key are created in the folder where you are (make sure you have write permissions to the folder) and you can then move the store wherever you want.

Now that you have this keystore, you can modify BUILD.JSON to use it like so:

```
{
    "android": {
        "release": {
            "keystore": "/home/MyKeys.keystore",
            "storePassword": "",
            "alias": "MyKeysAlias",
            "password" : ""
        }
    }
}
```

This ensures Cordova can find the store but I entered no passwords as I will be prompted during build and I won't have to show my passwords in a text file. So right now, if you would, let's issue a command to build the nTimer test app and sign it. The command is like this (on VSCODE terminal):

cordova build --release

A dialog pops up asking you for your store passwords (both the KeyStore and the Alias) as in this picture on the left.

When you enter your passwords, the application will resume building but this time it will be signed with your key and deployed to the build folder as android-release.apk (for Android). This APK could not be uploaded to a store. More on that below...

Application Stores

Application stores are a true blessing for those of us that, over the years, used to package and distribute applications on our own. In the old times, you had to find a publisher for your app (or distribute it directly from your site or a download site like CNET or

GameHippo) and you had to cater to all possible install scenarios (I remember writing installation files with NullSoft - a great piece of software) and then assuming that there are going to be no problems on the user/client side.

Today, you sign an application package (such as the above Android APK), log in to the store, specify a few things and done! Well there is a more detailed workflow (such as the store needs to approve your app which can take a while and also there are some guidelines for your app that you must comply with - more later) but overall this is really a piece of cake compared with how things used to be.

There are many stores (Google Play, Microsoft, AppStore from Apple, Amazon, BlackBerry, etc.). It is up to you which ones you want to send your app to but honestly, since Cordova targets all those stores, why not release the app for all?

You will need to have an account to be able to upload an app to a store. Most stores are free. I believe Google charges $50 as a one-time payment and about $100 or so for Apple but this is a tiny investment for the goodies you get. You even gate board-certified ratings for your app in most cases! A process that in the past would have been difficult and costly. This is where the stores are leveraging their aggregation power and economies of scale to help you out and this is most welcome!

So, for each store, you will need to create an account and set yourself up as a developer. Then, for every application submission, you will need to enter some required information so that the store can certify your app. In Windows, you can also use Microsoft's own App Certification Toolkit which is similar to the Windows Store and can pre-certify the app for you or at the very least, show you if there are going to be any problems.

Let's work through an example from google in the sections below because before you even plan on uploading your application package, you need to make sure you manifest and your assets are all good. Let's go over that check list now...

Examine Manifest

Unlike working with Android Studio where you can open the actual manifest, in Cordova you are working through CONFIG.XML which turns into a manifest. In fact, you can still access and modify the actual manifest from the build folders inside "platforms" but the more you can do with CONFIG.XML the safest things are and, I've never needed to modify an original manifest since CONFIG.XML does everything I need.

Let's do this one more time. Open CONFIG.XML in VSCODE and ensure that at least the following lines are altered:

```
<widget id="io.cordova.hellocordova"
version="1.0.0"
xmlns="http://www.w3.org/ns/widgets"
xmlns:cdv="http://cordova.apache.org/ns/1.0">
```

This line above needs to be changed to reflect your true app name and your version numbers like this: (note - every time you change your app version you need to change it here as well to be reflected in the manifest) ...

```
<widget id="com.madvox.nTimer" version="1.0.0"
xmlns="http://www.w3.org/ns/widgets"
xmlns:cdv="http://cordova.apache.org/ns/1.0">
```

Next, change all the obvious entries so they are correct (your name, your app name, your email address etc....):

```
<name>nTimer</name>
<description>
```

```
     A simple timer for educational purposes
</description>
<author                      email="admin@madvox.com"
href="http://www.madvox.com">
     The Madvox Team of One!
</author>
```

Next is the security section. Remember that if you leave it as it is by default, everything is accessible in your app from everywhere! So, it pays to remove lines you do not need and to grant explicit access to things you do need.

```
<access origin="*" />
<allow-intent href="http://*/*" />
<allow-intent href="https://*/*" />
<allow-intent href="tel:*" />
<allow-intent href="sms:*" />
<allow-intent href="mailto:*" />
<allow-intent href="geo:*" />
```

I am transforming the above to this:

```
<access origin="*" />
```

Because I do not need anything else at all for this app. But if you needed to access SMS or some web site API you would need to specify it here. Your application will not crash if you do not but the functionality will simply not work if you do not grant access to things like say, the weather forecast!

If you are going to use a Splash Screen you will need a plugin for that and the following lines:

```
<preference name="SplashScreen" value="screen" />
<preference name="FadeSplashScreen" value="false"
/>
```

You will also need to provide application images and assets for the store to display depending on different screen sizes and resolutions. Assets are all in a bunch of lines that look like this:

```
<platform name="android">
  <icon  src="logos/icons/android/icon-36-ldpi.png"
density="ldpi" />
  <icon  src="logos/icons/android/icon-48-mdpi.png"
density="mdpi" />
  <icon  src="logos/icons/android/icon-72-hdpi.png"
density="hdpi" />
  <icon src="logos/icons/android/icon-96-xhdpi.png"
density="xhdpi" />
</platform>
```

We have mentioned this before so make sure those png files are in the logos folder. I created the logos folder myself for simplicity but normally people put assets under a RES folder in platforms or another location. I just find it simpler to have all my assets together at root level that is all.

Stores have different requirements for assets so you will need to create icons and screenshots of your projects using different sizes and orientations. What each store needs, it will tell you at the time of filling up your application's page. Here are a couple of examples of what Windows and Android want to see (you will need to create these images and put them in CONFIG.XML):

Create a new app				Show/hide products	Filter	Search		
Name↑	Type	Included	Acquisitions	Feedback	Markets	Base price	Last modified	Status
MoonLock Jupiter	App	0 Add-ons	371 ↓	0	191	Free	10/3/2016	In the Store
MoonLock Saturn	App	0 Add-ons	326	0	191	Free	10/3/2016	In the Store
MXTimer	App	0 Add-ons	86 ↑	0	191	Free	6/27/2016	In the Store
nPuzzle	Game	0 Add-ons	286	0	2	Free	5/31/2016	In the Store
Oddnoid	Game	0 Add-ons	159	0	187	Free	5/31/2016	In the Store
Regolith	App	0 Add-ons	912	0	191	Free	3/4/2016	In the Store
TideLock	App	0 Add-ons	--	--	191	Free	12/17/2015	In progress

This last image above shows some of the screenshots I had to take to submit to the store for my app nTime.

The store asks you to upload images and it tells you the dimensions needed so you will need to get cracking and taking screenshots of your app and uploading them. You can actually take screenshots directly from the emulator which is a great time saver. There are also awesome applications that record your app live on the device. I usually submit at least one video too in order to show the user how the app works.

The above is an example of a video with a link if you want to examine it closer... (https://www.youtube.com/watch?v=BTVZcG0-RmE).

Application Assets

I mentioned above that you will need some screenshots of your app and also some promotional assets that are displayed in your personal store within Google Play or the AppStore. I am not very good at designing marketing or promotional materials but I am lucky to work with **Rospo Briccone** who excels at this and so he makes a lot of this stuff for me, including application icons, background, wallpapers, promotional materials, etc. If you need any of these I am sure he would give consideration to making them for you. He can be located here: **www.roguetoad27.com**.

If you decided to go at it yourself you will need:

1. An image editor like Paint Shop Pro, Adobe, Gimp or something similar;
2. Screenshot captures - many programs can do this including the emulator itself;
3. A lot of patience as there are many images required by the store.

In any case, do not forget to add images showing your app running in different devices (such as tablets, not just smartphones) because Google, for instance, will tag your app as only usable on phones if you do not supply tablet screenshots (and that does take you out of the tablet catalog which you do not want, if you can help it).

Please take the following advice: your application icon (the one displayed on the phone or tablet desktop when you install it) is specified in CONFIG.XML but I have had times when, for whatever reason, a default Cordova icon would show up. I never quite figured out why this happens occasionally but if this happens to you, the solution is to drop a copy of your app icon to the following folder(s): "platforms/android/res/". If you put your app icon there it will always be read fine! This is generally not needed but useful if your icon is not showing.

Google Dashboard Example

Let' show you how to upload an application to the Google Store. Remember, all stores are very similar so what you see here, with some minor differences, will be the same for most other stores…

First, create an account if you do not already have one and log on to the dashboard here: **https://play.g**

Once you log on, you are presented with a list of all the apps you have like the shot below:

App name	Price	Active / Total installs ⑦	Avg. rating / Total #	Crashes & ANRs ⑦	Last update	Status
MoonLock Jupiter 1.7.0	Free	70 / 335	★ 3.67 / 3	–	Feb 11, 2016	Published
MoonLock Saturn 1.7.0	Free	34 / 227	★ 5.00 / 2	–	Feb 11, 2016	Published
MXTimer 1.7.0	Free	15 / 116	★ 5.00 / 2	–	Feb 11, 2016	Published
nTime 1.2.9	Free	4 / 8	★ 5.00 / 1	–	Mar 17, 2017	Published
Oddnoid 1.3.4	Free	11 / 229	★ 3.33 / 3	–	Oct 29, 2014	Published
Regolith 1.9.5	Free	15 / 133	★ 5.00 / 2	–	Mar 3, 2016	Published
TideLock 2.0.8	Free	2 / 5	★ –	–	Apr 16, 2017	Published
WeightLock 1.7.0	Free	3 / 18	★ 1.00 / 1	–	Feb 11, 2016	Published

You can see some of my apps above with ratings and downloads. I admit I do this professionally but also a as hobby so I am not too worried with promotions. If you expect to make some money though, you should be!

From this dashboard, I can add or modify any app. I can modify and update to a newer version or create a new app. If you press the CREATE APPLICATION button you will be taken through all the necessary steps which are as follows:

- Store Listing - fill this section to provide an application name which must be unique, a short and full description, all the graphic assets you will need, promotional materials and videos, categories that your app fits in, etc.

- Content Rating: rating is required so fill in a survey to describe what the application does and you will be given a rating (including ESRB ratings!);

- After that, fill in your contact details. You must provide a privacy statement. You can use any of the many that are freely available on the web but you must provide a web page that explains how you handle privacy so users can check that out.

- After doing that, you can proceed to pricing and distribution. Unless you have encryption or sensitive functionality that your country (USA in my case) does not want you to export (in which case you have to exclude countries in the banned list) - you may choose all or any countries you want;

- Choose also the Google platforms you want your app to run in - this can be standard smartphones and tables or also Android Wear or TV's, even cars!

- There are options to opt-in to some nice programs such as children and family or education but you will need to fill surveys to ensure your app complies with those requirements;

- If you offer your app for free, no further questions in this section but if you plan to charge, you will need to provide a TAX identification number or your social security number so they can pay you and report to the IRS as required by law.

- There is also a section for in-app purchases if you have any. This is more and more common these days where for instance, the app is free but I can sell you modules within it to unlock additional features. Not a bad idea.

When you are done with this, you can proceed to RELEASE MANAGEMENT which is where you upload your APK.

Production   MANAGE PRODUCTION

Release: 1.7.0
Feb 11, 2016, 8:13 PM; Full rollout

Supported devices: **13679** Unsupported devices: **1665** Excluded devices: **0** Manage devices

1 APK version code: **107008**

You can see one of my apps in there as of release 1.7.0. This app supports a lower API level so many devices are supported. The number of devices supported will go up or down depending on your lowest supported API. These days, I do not go any lower than Android 4.1 and typically I would target Android 5 or higher because there are many great features starting with 5 and above and I do not want to appeal to the absolute minimum common denominator but this is your decision entirely.

In RELEASE MANAGEMENT, you can create new releases that will upgrade prior ones or, if you have none, it will create your very first release. It will bring up text from your store listing for description, author and such so making a release is very simple. Once you click the button you can drag and drop your RELEASE APK from your computer to this site. Once that is done, you can publish the app to PRODUCTION and Google takes a few hours to certify it and make sure everything is good and after that, everyone will see your app in the store.

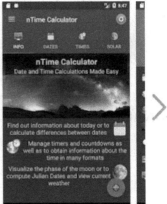

PERMISSION INFORMATION: nTime only requires permissions to access an Internet connection. The purpose of this permission is to retrieve the weather information from the National Oceanic and

The above listing is from my nTime application. You can see the full listing here:

https://play.google.com/store/apps/details?id=com.ntime.m advoxllc.ntime&hl=en

Promotion

Promotion is critical - if you have the best app in the world and nobody knows anything about it, it might as well not exist. I struggle with this all the time because I have some extremely accurate Astronomy applications and it is hard to position them where the people that would want it might see them. I have three pieces of advice on this:

1. If you really intend to make a living or make money from your apps, a good goal, then you can use old style marketing tips, contact someone that will promote your app, advertise, etc. That can get expensive but you will see results;

2. You may also keep the app free and put advertisements on it and let Google promote you through these ads. This does not give as much exposure as one might think but it is an option;

3. Finally, the best way in my view (perhaps combined with some bits from #1 above) is to promote it yourself. Get a Twitter or Facebook account, start talking about your app, target hashtags like #indieapps or #appsdev and start talking about your app. People will notice and will start talking about it to others.

I am not a marketing expert so I will let you consult the many experts out there. But I have had success with using Google Plus and Twitter. I love Twitter for the fast exposure and I love Google Plus since I can write a lot more and in a sense, blog about the app. Also, both programs allow you to embed your feed into your own web site if people prefer to visit you there.

Reviews, Rating and Feedback

I thought I would make a couple of remarks regarding Ratings and Reviews in particular. You can solicit feedback via the Google Play Store (it's built in) or you can put a feedback page on your app and let the users email you this feedback. I have done that in two of my apps. To be honest, you don't need it since people tend to provide feedback through the store but - it does not hurt to have that.

When it comes to Ratings and Reviews it is a jungle out there and so I want to point out some comments and advice I have for you, having done this over the years…

- Most people rate low - do not be discouraged by a 3 rating that is not a bad rating. Many people do not leave feedback as to why they rate you this way so it is a guessing game but, some do and it is incredibly useful. I had a user once that gave me a 2 rating because he did not know how to move the cursor on a game even though I had a help page for it. But I wrote back to the user, explained the process and he upgraded me to 5 instantly. It pays to communicate with your users;

- I hate 1-star reviews because most of the time when you get one star, the user did not understand what the app did or could not figure it out. Of course, it could also be that your app is crashing but in my experience, it is usually confusion that causes 1-star. I once had a user give me a one star on an app claiming that the app had the name "weight" on it but it wasn't a fitness app. And it wasn't, and I said so - people just don't read descriptions so you will need to think about that;

- Feedback pays off big time as I mentioned above. Encourage people to contact you and to leave feedback. It is so easy to clear up misunderstandings or even change functionality for the better due to good feedback. Do not be threatened for bad feedback - try to disarm the user with polite questions like - how would you like it to work? What can I do to make it better? - but I have received extremely constructive feedback that can be put to good use for all involved.

There is much more to say here but I just wanted to share some little pearls I learned over the years above anything else. If you expect to go viral and for people to flock to you and give you 5 stars all the time, you will be disappointed.

Google Developer Store

Google offers another good feature called the developer store where you can personalize your front-end to the user and promote some of your own applications. I love this feature.

Here is a screenshot of my developer store where I am promoting nTime. This shot is cropped - there is a lot more to show and all my other apps are gathered together here for my convenience and the user's.

Usage and Statistics

Finally, another thing I want to highlight about Google's Store is its detailed reports and statistics. You can access this from the main dashboard and there is even an application you can download to your mobile device to keep track of these as frequently as you want. Here are some screenshots of what I mean…

Plugins & Hooks

The last topic I want to cover is hooks and plugins. Let's start with hooks. A hook is a way provided by Cordova, for you to inject more code at certain automation points, thus allowing you even more freedom in the way Cordova commands are executed. Hooks are typically used to perform tasks before, during or after the execution of a Cordova command.

For instance, let's say you use a linter (linter are programs that are used to detect malformed code or other variety of errors or omissions or even to format your code in a special way). I typically use an HTML linter to ensure I do not have any malformed tags or other errors. The linter highlight these in its own output Window. So, let's say you want to make sure your code does not have any malformed tags and you want to run the linter just before building the app. A Cordova hook can be written to run "before build" and perhaps a formatter can be run "after build" to indent your code properly, just as an example.

So, as you can see, a hook is a placeholder in your app which, upon reached, will branch out and do some other task and then come back. Aside from indicating when a hook should run, a hook is written in JavaScript and placed in the "hooks" folder (although this has been deprecated now so you can place it wherever you want); you can specify that the hooks run directly from CONFIG.HTML.

Let me complete the example with our own test application nTimer. Let's say I want to run a hook and let's say I want to do that during the preparation phase, in case something goes wrong so that the build does not abort. Let my hook check for the presence of the android platform to see if this is an Android project or not.

I want to run this before preparation so, I will proceed to edit the CONFIG.XML file and do this:

```
<hook                           type="before_prepare"
src="hooks/checkAndroid.js" />
```

And here is the JS for this function (checkAndroid.JS):

```
module.exports = function(ctx) {
    if (ctx.opts.platforms.indexOf('android') < 0) {
      console.log('This  is  not  a  cordova  android
project");
        return;
    } else
      console.log("This    is    a    valid    Android
project");
};
```

Using Plugins

Remember that Cordova has a huge number of plugins. This is a reminder that you can include plugins in your CONFIG.XML from people that have already written useful ones, including the Apache Cordova Team. I showed you how to insert plugins in earlier sections so this is just a reminder.

Full Example Application: nTimer - a Lap Timer

It is time to write a proper app. We are going to finish our skeletal nTimer app. It will be a simple app but it will be created professionally and it will contain useful functionality. There are many apps like this one but the purpose here is not to invent something new but to give you a good working ap.

Here is what you can expect:

1. Forward counter (lap counter);
2. Countdown (back counter);
3. Sharing laps with others;
4. Using JQuery for navigation and CSS;
5. Using HTML5 for putting the UI together;
6. Using JavaScript ESS6 for coding;
7. Full Settings Page;
8. Navigation Drawer required for some devices;
9. Using some plugins that we need;
10. Using a third-party library for circular gauges;
11. Two different views: using circular gauges or just digital clock;
12. Keep the app alive in the background so timers keep going;
13. Using sounds for timers;
14. Proper code structure, version control and other professional features.

We will design and write each part of this application in the proper order to illustrate how you can focus on the UI and only when you are happy with it can you then move to the code.

In order to avoid listing a huge application here I will simply highlight the most important code pieces and will give you a link (in the appendix) to download the full source at your convenience.

First things first though - remember to create a GIT repository for this project as I am - revisit the earlier chapter on that topic if you have not done that already. I will be making references to staging and committing files so I do not want you to get lost with that. Although it is optional if you wish to skip it.

Design the UI: CSS and HTML

We are going to start working on INDEX.HTML and our CSS files so that we can design what the UI looks like. I am giving you a flavour of a good UI here but please feel free to change it into whatever looks you want. There isn't a single UI possible for a program like this - you have many choices. But I am keeping things simple not to get you lost in design choices.

So, let's say state that we are going to be using JQUERY mobile for this application as well as Cordova of course. When it comes to mixing JQuery and Cordova you need to make sure you include your stylesheets and your JavaScript in a specific order - this order is important. So, before we do anything else, let's create a template, blank INDEX.HTML file that will work with Cordova and JQuery mobile...

```
<!DOCTYPE html>
<html>
```

```html
<head>
    <meta charset="utf-8" />
    <meta http-equiv="Content-Security-Policy"
content="default-src 'self' data: gap:
https://ssl.gstatic.com 'unsafe-eval'; style-src
'self' 'unsafe-inline'; media-src *">

    <title>nTimer</title>
    <meta http-equiv="Content-type"
content="text/html; charset=utf-8" />
    <meta name="viewport" content="user-
scalable=yes, initial-scale=1, maximum-scale=1,
minimum-scale=1, width=device-width" />


    <link href="css/jquery.mobile-1.4.5.min.css"
rel="stylesheet" type="text/css" />
    <link href="css/Madvox.min.css"
rel="stylesheet" type="text/css" />
    <link href="css/colorPicker.css"
rel="stylesheet" type="text/css" />


    <!-- Framework Scripts -->
    <script
src="scripts/Frameworks/jquery.min.js"></script>
    <script
src="scripts/Initialize.js"></script>
  </head>


  <body>


    <!-- Cordova reference, this is added to
your app when it's built. -->
    <script src="cordova.js"></script>
    <script src="scripts/index.js"></script>
    <script
src="scripts/Frameworks/jquery.min.js"></script>
```

```
        <script
src="scripts/Frameworks/jquery.mobile-
1.4.5.min.js"></script>
        <script
src="scripts/Frameworks/jquery.colorPicker.min.js">
</script>
        <script src="scripts/cStartup.js"></script>
        <script src="scripts/cTimer.js"></script>
        <script src="scripts/Down.js"></script>


    </body>


</html>
```

The above is a perfectly valid blank INDEX.HTML template for Cordova. It does not do anything but feel free to run it (you will see a blank page). Let's explain important concepts here:

```
        <meta http-equiv="Content-Security-Policy"
content="default-src 'self' data: gap:
https://ssl.gstatic.com 'unsafe-eval'; style-src
'self' 'unsafe-inline'; media-src *">
```

The above is your content security policy. You can go to the **CSP** web site for a good intro on what this is but I will explain here that this is important protection for your code. How you configure it is up to you but I tend to use "self" and "unsafe-eval" to indicate that code or requests not originating from my own files is not allowed to run at all. You may use "unsafe-inline" to allow scripts to run inline (recall our definitions earlier) but this is a riskier approach to "unsafe-eval". I do feel that styles are ok inline but code is definitely not.

```
        <link href="css/jquery.mobile-1.4.5.min.css"
rel="stylesheet" type="text/css" />
        <link href="css/Madvox.min.css"
rel="stylesheet" type="text/css" />
```

```html
      <link href="css/colorPicker.css"
rel="stylesheet" type="text/css" />


      <!-- Framework Scripts -->
      <script
src="scripts/Frameworks/jquery.min.js"></script>
      <script
src="scripts/Initialize.js"></script>
```

The code above inserts the stylesheets needed for JQuery and its plug ins. Note that JQuery Mobile is the first stylesheet included and Madvox is just my theme roller for JQuery for this app so I can choose from a few themes. Finally, the colorpicker is also a jQuery plugin that allows you to pick colors for your fonts etc. So, as you can see, in this app, I have no CSS of my own. I am using JQuery for everything.

Also, you must include JQuery initialization scripts in the header part of your code which is why you see jquery.min.js and an initialization script of my own to kick off JQuery right away.

```html
      <!-- Cordova reference, this is added to
your app when it's built. -->
      <script src="cordova.js"></script>
      <script src="scripts/index.js"></script>
      <script
src="scripts/Frameworks/jquery.min.js"></script>
      <script
src="scripts/Frameworks/jquery.mobile-
1.4.5.min.js"></script>
      <script
src="scripts/Frameworks/jquery.colorPicker.min.js">
</script>
      <script src="scripts/cStartup.js"></script>
      <script src="scripts/cTimer.js"></script>
      <script src="scripts/Down.js"></script>
```

Finally, as illustrated above, at the very end of your file, before closing the body tag, you can include all other scripts both the Cordova scripts (cordova.js and index.js) as well as the remaining JQuery Mobile ones and your own. My own scripts are the last three.

So now you have a standard INDEX.HTML that can be filled up with your custom UI and the CSS are provided by JQuery so you are ready to start. Let's create a UI now then by continuing to fill in INDEX.HTML:

The code below represents the HTML code between the two body tags - all of it....

```html
<!-- Sounds →
<audio id="secondTick" src="sounds/Clock.wav"
typeof="audio/wav"></audio>
<audio id="bellSound" src="sounds/Bell.wav"
typeof="audio/wav"></audio>
<audio id="gongSound" src="sounds/gong.wav"
typeof="audio/wav"></audio>
<audio id="knockSound" src="sounds/knock.wav"
typeof="audio/wav"></audio>


<!-- Entry Page -->

    <div data-role="page" data-theme="a" data-
title="MXTimer" id="index">
        <div data-role="header">
            <h1>MADVOX TIMER</h1>
        </div>

        <div data-role="content">
            <div class="ui-grid-a">
                <div class="ui-block-a">
                    <div class="ui-bar">
```

```html
                        <a href="#STWatch"><img
src="images/count.png" /></a>
                        <p style="text-
align:center;"><label
id="lChrono">CHRONOMETER</label></p>
                    </div>
                </div>
                <div class="ui-block-b">
                    <div class="ui-bar">
                        <a href="#STCount"><img
src="images/clock.png" /></a>
                        <p style="text-
align:center;"><label
id="lDown">COUNTDOWN</label></p>
                    </div>
                </div>
            </div>
            <div class="ui-grid-solo">
                <div class="ui-block-a">
                    <div class="ui-bar">
                        <a href="#STData"><img
src="images/data.png" /></a>
                        <p style="text-
align:center;">DATA ANALYSIS</p>
                    </div>
                </div>
            </div>
        </div>


        <div data-role="footer" data-
position="fixed">
            <div data-role="navbar">
                <ul>
                    <li><a href="#STWatch" data-
icon="clock">Chrono</a></li>
                    <li><a href="#STCount" data-
icon="carat-d">Down</a></li>
                    <li><a href="#STData" data-
icon="bars">Data</a></li>
```

```html
                    <li><a href="#MXOptions" data-
icon="gear">Options</a></li>
                </ul>
            </div>
        </div>
    </div>


    <!-- Stop Watch Page -->

    <div data-role="page" data-theme="a" data-
title="StopWatch" id="STWatch">
        <div data-role="header">
            <h1>CHRONOMETER</h1>
            <img src="images/count.png" class="ui-
btn-right" style="height: 32px; width: 26px;" />
        </div>


        <div data-role="content">
            <center>
                <div class="ui-grid-b">
                    <div class="ui-bar">
                        <div class="stopwatch" data-
autostart="false">
                            <div class=" time">
                                <span
class="hours"></span><span class="hdots">:</span>
                                <span
class="minutes"></span><span class="mdots">:</span>
                                <span
class="seconds"></span><span class="sdots">:</span>
                                <span
class="milliseconds"></span>
                            </div>
                            <div class="controls">
                            </div>
                        </div>
                    </div>
```

```html
            <div>
                <div class="gap">
                    <div class=" time">
                         
                    </div>
                </div>
            </div>
            <div class="ui-bar">
                <div class="BestLap">
                    <strong>Best
Lap</strong> <span class="bcLap"
id="bestLapTime"></span>
                </div>
                <ul data-role="listview"
id="lapListHead" data-inset="true">
                    <li><img
src="images/bell.png" class="ui-li-icon">
                        <div>Lap / Diff.
<span class="cLap"></span><span class="ui-li-
count">Lap Time</span></div>
                    </li>
                </ul>
                <ul data-role="listview"
id="lapList" data-inset="true"></ul>


            </div>
        </div>
    </center>

</div>


    <div data-role="footer" data-
position="fixed" class="controlButtons">
        <div data-role="navbar">
            <ul>
                <li><a href="#index" data-
icon="home">Home</a></li>
```

```
                        <li><a class="reset" data-
icon="forbidden">Reset</a></li>
                        <li><a class="lap" data-
icon="tag">Lap</a></li>
                        <li><a class="toggle" data-
icon="clock" data-pausetext="Pause" data-
resumetext="Resume">Start</a></li>
                </ul>
            </div>
        </div>
    </div>


    <!-- CountDown Page  -->

    <div data-role="page" data-theme="a" data-
title="Countdown" id="STCount">
        <div data-role="header">
            <h1>COUNTDOWN</h1>
            <img src="images/clock.png" class="ui-
btn-right" style="height: 32px; width: 26px;" />
        </div>

        <div data-role="content">
            <center>
                <div class="ui-grid-b">
                    <div class="ui-bar">
                        <div class="scountdown">
                            <div class="scount">
                                <span
class="ctime"></span>
                            </div>
                            <div class="controls">
                            </div>
                        </div>
                    </div>
                </div>
                <div>
```

```html
<form>
    <h3>Set Timer</h3>
    <div class="ui-checkbox">
        <label for="checkbox-
enhanced" class="ui-btn ui-corner-all ui-btn-
inherit ui-btn-icon-left ui-checkbox-
off">Loop/Repeat</label>
        <input type="checkbox"
name="cLoop" id="cLoop" data-enhanced="true">
    </div>
    <div class="ui-field-
contain" id="cDownSliders">
        <label
for="hourSlider">Hours</label>
        <input type="range"
name="hourSlider" id="hourSlider" min="0" max="24"
value="0" data-highlight="true">
        <label
for="minSlider">Minutes</label>
        <input type="range"
name="minSlider" id="minSlider" min="0" max="59"
value="1" data-highlight="true">
        <label
for="secSlider">Seconds</label>
        <input type="range"
name="secSlider" id="secSlider" min="0" max="59"
value="0" data-highlight="true">
    </div>
</form>
        </div>
    </center>
</div>


<div data-role="footer" data-
position="fixed" class="controlButtons">
    <div data-role="navbar">
        <ul>
            <li><a href="#index" data-
icon="home">Home</a></li>
```

```
                        <li><a class="cdreset" data-
icon="forbidden">Reset</a></li>
                        <li><a class="cdtoggle" data-
icon="clock" data-cdpausetext="Pause" data-
cdresumetext="Resume">Start</a></li>
                </ul>
            </div>
        </div>
    </div>


<!-- Data Page -->

    <div data-role="page" data-theme="a" data-
title="History" id="STData">
        <div data-role="header">
            <h1>TIME DATA</h1>
            <img src="images/data.png" class="ui-
btn-right" style="height: 32px; width: 26px;" />
        </div>


        <div data-role="content">
            <button class="ui-btn"
id="LapResults">Load Last Time Set</button>
            <ul data-role="listview" data-
filter="true" id="LapHistory"></ul>
        </div>


        <div data-role="footer" data-
position="fixed" class="controlButtons">
            <div data-role="navbar">
                <ul>
                    <li><a href="#index" data-
icon="home">Home</a></li>
                    <li><a class="share" data-
icon="comment" id="oShare">Share</a></li>
                </ul>
```

```
          </div>
        </div>
    </div>


<!-- Options Page -->


    <div data-role="page" data-theme="a" data-
title="Options" id="MXOptions">
        <div data-role="header">
            <h1>APP OPTIONS</h1>
            <img src="images/gear.png" class="ui-
btn-right" style="height: 32px; width: 32px;" />
        </div>


        <div data-role="content">
            <form>
                <div class="ui-field-contain">
                    <fieldset data-
role="controlgroup" data-type="horizontal">
                        <legend>App
Theme</legend><span class="cTheme"></span>
                        <input type="radio"
name="radioTheme" id="radio-choice-a" value="a"
data-theme="a" /><label for="radio-choice-
a"></label>
                        <input type="radio"
name="radioTheme" id="radio-choice-b" value="b"
data-theme="b" /><label for="radio-choice-
b"></label>
                        <input type="radio"
name="radioTheme" id="radio-choice-c" value="c"
data-theme="c" /><label for="radio-choice-
c"></label>
                        <input type="radio"
name="radioTheme" id="radio-choice-d" value="d"
data-theme="d" /><label for="radio-choice-
d"></label>
```

```html
                            <input type="radio"
name="radioTheme" id="radio-choice-e" value="e"
data-theme="e" /><label for="radio-choice-
e"></label>
                            <input type="radio"
name="radioTheme" id="radio-choice-f" value="f"
data-theme="f" /><label for="radio-choice-
f"></label>
                            <input type="radio"
name="radioTheme" id="radio-choice-g" value="g"
data-theme="g" /><label for="radio-choice-
g"></label>
                    </fieldset>
                </div>


                <div class="ui-field-contain">
                    <ul data-role="listview" data-
inset="true">
                        <li>
                            <label
for="oFontColor">Font Color</label>
                            <input id="oFontColor"
type="text" name="oFontColor" value="#000" />
                        </li>
                    </ul>
                </div>


                <div class="ui-field-contain">
                    <label for="slider0">Font
Size</label>
                    <input type="range"
name="slider0" id="slider0" value="1" min="1"
max="5" data-highlight="true" />
                </div>


                <div class="ui-field-contain">
                    <label for="slider2">Keep
Alive</label>
```

```
                      <select id="slider2"
name="slider2" data-role="flipswitch">
                         <option
value="on">on</option>
                         <option
value="off">off</option>
                      </select>
                   </div>


                   <div class="ui-field-contain">
                      <label
for="slider3">Vibrate</label>
                      <select id="slider3"
name="slider3" data-role="flipswitch">
                         <option
value="on">on</option>
                         <option
value="off">off</option>
                      </select>
                   </div>


                   <div style="float:right;"><br
/><label>Click <strong>apply</strong> to save
settings</label></div>
                </form>
         </div>


      <div data-role="footer" data-
position="fixed" class="controlButtons">
         <div data-role="navbar">
            <ul>
               <li><a href="#index" data-
icon="home">Home</a></li>
               <li><a class="apply" data-
icon="check" id="oApply">Apply</a></li>
            </ul>
         </div>
      </div>
```

```
        </div>
```

In addition to adding some sound for later use, this entire INDEX.HTML section is defining pages that you can navigate to. They are all the same but they contain different things so let's take a look at that we are trying to do here by looking at one page. The very first page is the menu and it has the following code:

```
    <div data-role="page" data-theme="a" data-
title="MXTimer" id="index">
        <div data-role="header">
            <h1>MADVOX TIMER</h1>
        </div>


        <div data-role="content">
            <div class="ui-grid-a">
                <div class="ui-block-a">
                    <div class="ui-bar">
                        <a href="#STWatch"><img
src="images/count.png" /></a>
                        <p style="text-
align:center;"><label
id="lChrono">CHRONOMETER</label></p>
                    </div>
                </div>
                <div class="ui-block-b">
                    <div class="ui-bar">
                        <a href="#STCount"><img
src="images/clock.png" /></a>
                        <p style="text-
align:center;"><label
id="lDown">COUNTDOWN</label></p>
                    </div>
                </div>
            </div>
            <div class="ui-grid-solo">
                <div class="ui-block-a">
                    <div class="ui-bar">
```

```
                    <a href="#STData"><img
src="images/data.png" /></a>
                        <p style="text-
align:center;">DATA ANALYSIS</p>
                </div>
            </div>
        </div>
      </div>


      <div data-role="footer" data-
position="fixed">
            <div data-role="navbar">
                <ul>
                    <li><a href="#STWatch" data-
icon="clock">Chrono</a></li>
                    <li><a href="#STCount" data-
icon="carat-d">Down</a></li>
                    <li><a href="#STData" data-
icon="bars">Data</a></li>
                    <li><a href="#MXOptions" data-
icon="gear">Options</a></li>
                </ul>
            </div>
        </div>
    </div>
```

A JQuery Page has three sections: a header (data-role header), contents (data-role content) and a footer (data-role footer). Except for the content part the other two are optional but nice because they allow you to have a page title and buttons at the bottom for additional actions. This many page allows you access to a grid of icons that will take you to a Lap Timer page, or a Countdown Page or some Analytics page.

There are shortcuts in the footer for quick access to for instance, Settings.

All the other pages are the same but they vary in content. The Settings page is very simple - it allows you to choose a color for the font, font sizes and themes. You can customize this page to do anything else you want (such as whether sounds are on or off, or whether the timers should be circular or digital, etc.)

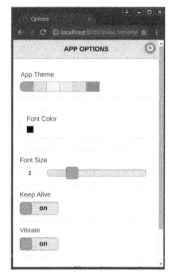

On the right, I am showing you the options (settings) window except I changed the theme so that you can get a feel for how you can use different colors and sizes in your apps.

As I mentioned above, the other pages are the same but the content is different. Whenever you click on an icon from the menu, navigation is redirected to the target page via a simple # tag because I am using SPA so all pages are in the same INDEX.HTML.

So, by specifying an HREF='#PageName' you can go to that page - it is that simple.

So, you can see how you can spend your time designing your UI fully until you are happy with it (I have not written a single line of code yet) before you write any code. This is great because the UI is entirely decoupled from the code and so even after you write the code you can still mess with the UI with no consequences.

Design the Code

So, what about the code? Well let's make a distinction between framework or cordova code and your own. The framework code (in our case JQuery and plugins) has already been inserted above so no more to do there. In the case of Cordova, the index.js file was created by it. You can inspect this file (see below) and notice how it is just initializing Cordova. You do have events to insert code if the application is paused or terminated or resumed.

```
(function () {
    "use strict";

    document.addEventListener('deviceready',
onDeviceReady.bind(this), false);

    function onDeviceReady() {
        // Handle the Cordova pause and resume
events
        document.addEventListener('pause',
onPause.bind(this), false);
        document.addEventListener('resume',
onResume.bind(this), false);
    };

    function onPause() {
        // TODO: This application has been
suspended. Save application state here.
    };

    function onResume() {
        // TODO: This application has been
reactivated. Restore application state here.
    };
})();
```

You may leave this file alone for the most part - everything will work fine without making changes here at least until you have a specific need to do something with it which, for nTimer, we do not.

So, then there is your code. I tend to put the framework code in a FRAMEWORKS folder and my own code in a SCRIPTS folder to keep them separate. I have only three code files:

- StartUp.js: Initializes the code and sets up the pages;
- cTimer.js: This is the lap timer;
- Down.js: This is the Countdown.

So, we write our personal files inside the SCRIPTS folder and we are good to go. Let's discuss these files.

Start-up Code File

I use this file to initialize everything and for the most part it is self-explanatory. Take a look below (note I wrote this quickly so you can probably organize the code a bit better but it does its job well):

```
var s_appTheme = "a";
var s_fontColor = "#0000ff";
var s_fontSize = 1;
var s_keepAlive = 'off';
var s_vibrate = 'off';
var FontScale = 24;


$.mobile.defaultPageTransition = "slide";


$.mobile.changeGlobalTheme = function (theme) {
    var themes = " a b c d e f g";


    try {
        function setTheme(cssSelector, themeClass,
theme) {
            $(cssSelector)
                .removeClass(themes.split("
").join(" " + themeClass + "-"))
```

```
                .addClass(themeClass + "-" + theme)
                .attr("data-theme", theme);
        }

        setTheme("[data-role='page']", "ui-body",
theme);
    } catch (e) {


    }
};


function ChangeTheme() {
    try {
        if ((s_appTheme != "a") && (s_appTheme !=
"b") && (s_appTheme != "c") && (s_appTheme != "d")
&& (s_appTheme != "e") && (s_appTheme != "f") &&
(s_appTheme != "g"))
            s_appTheme = "a";
        $.mobile.changeGlobalTheme(s_appTheme);
    } catch (e) {


    }
}


function Vibrate(totaltime) {
    try {
        if (s_vibrate === 'on')
                navigator.vibrate(totaltime);
    } catch (e) {


    }
}


$(function () {

    try {
```

```
        var applyElement =
$('.controlButtons').find('.apply');
        var targetTheme = "a";


        applyElement.on('click', function () {


            var Value = $('#slider2').val();
            if (Value === 'on')
window.plugins.insomnia.keepAwake();
            if (Value === 'off')
window.plugins.insomnia.allowSleepAgain();


            storeSettings();
            targetTheme =
$('input[name=radioTheme]:checked').val();
            s_appTheme = targetTheme;


            ChangeTheme();
            ChangeCSS();
            $.mobile.changePage('#index');
        });
    } catch (e) {


    }


});


$(function () {
    $('#oFontColor').colorPicker({ showHexField:
false });
});


function setDefaults() {
```

```
    try {
        $('#slider0').val(s_fontSize);
$('#slider0').slider('refresh');
        $('#oFontColor').val(s_fontColor);
$('#oFontColor').change();
        $('#slider2').val(s_keepAlive);
$('#slider2').flipswitch('refresh');
        $('#slider3').val(s_vibrate);
$('#slider3').flipswitch('refresh');
        $("input[name='" + "radioTheme" +
"'][value='" + s_appTheme + "']").prop('checked',
true);
    } catch (e) {
    }
}

function removeSettings() {
    try {
        localStorage.removeItem('appTheme');
        localStorage.removeItem('fontColor');
        localStorage.removeItem('fontSize');
        localStorage.removeItem('keepAlive');
        localStorage.removeItem('vibrate');

        setDefaults();
    } catch (e) {

    }
}

function storeSettings() {
    try {
        if ('localStorage' in window &&
window['localStorage'] !== null) {
            try {
                s_appTheme =
$('input[name=radioTheme]:checked').val();
```

```
                    s_fontColor =
$('#oFontColor').val();
                    s_fontSize = $('#slider0').val();
                    s_keepAlive = $('#slider2').val();
                    s_vibrate = $('#slider3').val();

                    localStorage.setItem('appTheme',
s_appTheme);
                    localStorage.setItem('fontColor',
s_fontColor);
                    localStorage.setItem('fontSize',
s_fontSize);
                    localStorage.setItem('keepAlive',
s_keepAlive);
                    localStorage.setItem('vibrate',
s_vibrate);
                } catch (e) {
                    alert('Unable to save settings!');
                }
            } else {
                alert('Storage is not allowed!');
            }
        } catch (e) {

        }
}


function ApplyInitialSettings() {

    try {
        if (localStorage.length != 0) {
                s_appTheme =
localStorage.getItem('appTheme');
                s_fontColor =
localStorage.getItem('fontColor');
                s_fontSize =
localStorage.getItem('fontSize');
```

```
            s_keepAlive =
localStorage.getItem('keepAlive');
            s_vibrate =
localStorage.getItem('vibrate');
            ChangeTheme();
        } else {
            setDefaults();
        }
    } catch (e) {

    }
}


function useSettings() {

    try {
        if (localStorage.length != 0) {
            s_appTheme =
localStorage.getItem('appTheme');
            s_fontColor =
localStorage.getItem('fontColor');
            s_fontSize =
localStorage.getItem('fontSize');
            s_keepAlive =
localStorage.getItem('keepAlive');
            s_vibrate =
localStorage.getItem('vibrate');


            $('#slider0').val(s_fontSize);
$('#slider0').slider('refresh');
            $('#oFontColor').val(s_fontColor);
$('#oFontColor').change();
            $('#slider2').val(s_keepAlive);
$('#slider2').flipswitch('refresh');
            $('#slider3').val(s_vibrate);
$('#slider3').flipswitch('refresh');
```

```
            $("input[name='" + "radioTheme" +
"'][value='" + s_appTheme + "']").prop('checked',
true);
            ChangeTheme();

        } else {
            setDefaults();
            ChangeTheme();
        }
    } catch (e) {


    }
}


function ChangeCSS() {
    try {
        $('.scountdown').find('.ctime').css('color',
s_fontColor);
        $('.scountdown').find('.ctime').css('font-
size', s_fontSize * FontScale + "px");


        $('.stopwatch').find('.hours').css('font-
size', s_fontSize * FontScale + 'px');
        $('.stopwatch').find('.minutes').css('font-
size', s_fontSize * FontScale + 'px');
        $('.stopwatch').find('.seconds').css('font-
size', s_fontSize * FontScale + 'px');


        $('.stopwatch').find('.hdots').css('font-
size', s_fontSize * FontScale + 'px');
        $('.stopwatch').find('.mdots').css('font-
size', s_fontSize * FontScale + 'px');
        $('.stopwatch').find('.sdots').css('font-
size', s_fontSize * FontScale + 'px');


        $('.stopwatch').find('.hours').css('color',
s_fontColor);
```

```javascript
        $('.stopwatch').find('.minutes').css('color'
, s_fontColor);
        $('.stopwatch').find('.seconds').css('color'
, s_fontColor);
        $('.stopwatch').find('.milliseconds').css('c
olor', s_fontColor);
    } catch (e) {


    }
}

$(document).on("pagecreate", "#index", function
(event) {
    ApplyInitialSettings();
});

$(document).on("pagecreate", "#MXOptions", function
(event) {
    useSettings();
});

$(document).on("pagecreate", "#STWatch", function
(event) {
    ChangeCSS();
});

$(document).on("pagecreate", "#STCount", function
(event) {
    ChangeCSS();
});

$(document).on("pagecreate", "#STData", function
(event) {
    ChangeCSS();
});
```

Some highlights with this code:

- It sets up default variables for our settings such as font colors, theme names, etc.;
- It provides a function to change the global theme when the user requests it;
- It has a vibrate function if the user prefers no sounds;
- It displays the color picker when needed;
- It saves and retrieves our settings from internal device storage;
- It initializes pages through the JQuery at the OnPageCreate event before they are displayed.

It is your basic initialization. As I mentioned before, you can probably structure this code much better. I am just putting it together as a good demo for you from a bunch of my own apps and that obviously shows but the code works quite well.

Lap Timer Code File

The Lap Timer starts and stops a counter and it allows you to record laps. The best laps are highlighted and lap differences are shown. You can access the Analytics options in the main menu just after a lap session to see and share details about this. If you were running on a track for instance, you could take milestone laps and then share the whole results.

```
$(function () {

    var toggleElement =
$('.controlButtons').find('.toggle');
    var resetElement =
$('.controlButtons').find('.reset');
```

```
    var lapElement =
$('.controlButtons').find('.lap');
    var pauseText = toggleElement.data('pausetext');
    var resumeText =
toggleElement.data('resumetext');
    var startText = toggleElement.text();
    var currentLap = 0;
    var MaxLaps = 256;
    var prevLap = "00:00:00:000";
    var bestLap = "00:00:00:000";
    var lapSplit;
    var prevSplit = "00:00:00:000";
    var topLap = 3600;
    var highLap = -1;
    var topLapLine = "";
    var rTime = [];
    var rLap = [];
    var rSplit = [];


    $('.stopwatch').each(function () {


        // Cache very important elements, especially
the ones used always
        var element = $(this);
        var running = element.data('autostart');
        var hoursElement = element.find('.hours');
        var minutesElement =
element.find('.minutes');
        var secondsElement =
element.find('.seconds');
        var millisecondsElement =
element.find('.milliseconds');

        function InitializeArrays() {
            var i = 0;

            for (i = 0; i < MaxLaps; i++) {
```

```
                    rTime[i] = "nop";
                    rLap[i] = "nop";
                    rSplit[i] = "nop";
                }
            }


        function GetMessage() {
                var Content = "";
                var n = 0;
                var DataDate = new Date();
                var CurrentStamp = "Shared on: " +
(DataDate.getMonth() + 1) + "/"
                            + DataDate.getDate() +
"/"
                            + DataDate.getFullYear()
+ " @ "
                            + DataDate.getHours() +
":"
                            + DataDate.getMinutes()
+ ":"
                            + DataDate.getSeconds();

            if (rTime[0] === "nop")
                return ("No Time Data Available");

            Content = "MXTimer Application time
data.\n(<<) Indicates best lap.\n"
            Content += CurrentStamp + "\n\n";
            Content += "LAP | CLOCK / TIME | LAP
TIME | DELTA\n";

            for (n = 0; n < MaxLaps; n++) {
                if (rTime[n] === "nop")
                    break;
```

```javascript
                Content += prependZero(n + 1, 3) + "
 | " + rTime[n] + " | " + rLap[n] + " | " +
rSplit[n];
                if (n == highLap - 1) Content += "
<<";

                Content += "\n";
            }
        //$('#LapHistory').prepend('<li data-
role="list-divider">LAP | CLOCK / TIME | LAP TIME |
DELTA</li>').listview('refresh');
            return (Content);
        }


    function ShowArrays() {
        var Content = "";
        var n = 0;
        var Highlight = "inherit";
        var bgString = "background-color:
#ffff99";
        var BestLapTime = "";


        $('#LapHistory').empty();


        if (rTime[0] === "nop") {
            $('#LapHistory').prepend('<li>End of
Results</li>').listview('refresh');
            return;
        }


        BestLapTime = rLap[highLap - 1];

        for (n = 0; n < MaxLaps; n++) {
            if (rTime[n] === "nop")
                break;


            //rSplit[n] =
TimeDifference(rLap[n], BestLapTime, true, true);
```

```
                if (rSplit[n].indexOf("-") == 0)
Highlight = "green";
                if (rSplit[n].indexOf("+") == 0)
Highlight = "red";


            Content = prependZero(n + 1, 3) + "
| " + rTime[n] + " | " + rLap[n] + " | " +
rSplit[n];


            if (n == highLap-1) Highlight += ";
" + bgString;


            $('#LapHistory').prepend('<li
style="color: ' + Highlight + ';">' + Content +
'</li>').listview('refresh');


        }
        $('#LapHistory').prepend('<li data-
role="list-divider">LAP | CLOCK / TIME | LAP TIME |
DELTA</li>').listview('refresh');
        Highlight = "inherit";
    }


    function Record(t1) {
        var nm1, ns1, nl1;

        nm1 = parseInt(t1.split(':')[0], 10);
        ns1 = parseInt(t1.split(':')[1], 10);
        nl1 = parseInt(t1.split(':')[2], 10);

        var tt1 = nm1 * 60 + ns1 + nl1 / 1000;
        if (tt1 < topLap) {
            topLap = tt1;
            return true;
        }
    }
```

```
        return false;
    }

    function Compress(t1) {
        var nm, ns, nl;
        var str = "";

        nm = parseInt(t1.split(':')[0], 10);
        ns = parseInt(t1.split(':')[1], 10);
        nl = parseInt(t1.split(':')[2], 10);

        if (nm != 0) str += prependZero(nm,2) +
":";
        if (ns != 0) str += prependZero(ns,2);
        if (nl != 0) str += "." +
prependZero(nl,3);

        return (str);

    }

    function RecalculateSplits(referenceLap) {
        $('#lapList li').each(function () {
            var Row = $(this).find('.lLap');
            var Value = $(this).find('.gLap');
            var KeyLap = $(this).find('.cLap');

            if (referenceLap != "00:00:00:000")
{
                lapDelta = TimeDifference("00:"
+ referenceLap, "00:" + Value.text(), true, true);
                Row.text(lapDelta);

                $(this).css('background-color',
'inherit');

                Row.css('color', 'red');
```

```javascript
                    Value.css('color', 'inherit');
                    KeyLap.css('color', 'inherit');
                    if (lapDelta.length <= 0) {
                        $(this).css('background-
color', '#ffff99');
                    }
                }
            });
        }


        function TimeDifference(t1, t2, usesign,
forcesign) {
            var Negative = false;

            var hourDiff =
parseInt(t1.split(':')[0], 10) -
parseInt(t2.split(':')[0], 10);
            var minDiff = parseInt(t1.split(':')[1],
10) - parseInt(t2.split(':')[1], 10);
            var secDiff = parseInt(t1.split(':')[2],
10) - parseInt(t2.split(':')[2], 10);
            var milliDiff =
parseInt(t1.split(':')[3], 10) -
parseInt(t2.split(':')[3], 10);

            if (hourDiff < 0 || minDiff < 0 ||
secDiff < 0 || milliDiff < 0)
                Negative = true;

            hourDiff = Math.abs(hourDiff);
            minDiff = Math.abs(minDiff);
            secDiff = Math.abs(secDiff);
            milliDiff = Math.abs(milliDiff);

            hourDiff = prependZero(hourDiff,2);
minDiff = prependZero(minDiff,2);   secDiff =
```

```
prependZero(secDiff,2); milliDiff =
prependZero(milliDiff,3);


          //var totalDiff = hourDiff + ":" +
minDiff + ":" + secDiff + ":" + milliDiff;
          var totalDiff = minDiff + ":" + secDiff
+ ":" + milliDiff;


          if (usesign) totalDiff =
Compress(totalDiff);


          if (usesign) {
              if (forcesign) {
                  totalDiff = "+" + totalDiff;
              } else {
                  if (Negative)
                      totalDiff = "-" + totalDiff;
                  else
                      totalDiff = "+" + totalDiff;


              }
              if (totalDiff.length <= 1)
                  totalDiff = "";
          }

          return (totalDiff);
      }


      function AddLap() {
          $('#lapList').prepend('<li><img
src="images/lapdata.png" class="ui-li-icon"><div
class="gap"><span class="cLap"></span><span
class="lLap"></span><span class="ui-li-count"><span
class="gLap"></span></span></div></li>').listview('
refresh');
          var cLapElement = $('#lapList
li').first().find('.cLap');
```

```
            var gLapElement = $('#lapList
li').first().find('.gLap');
            var lLapElement = $('#lapList
li').first().find('.lLap');


            var LapText = prependZero(hours,
2).toString() + ":" + prependZero(minutes,
2).toString() + ":" + prependZero(seconds,
2).toString() + ":" + prependZero(milliseconds,
3).toString();
            lapSplit = TimeDifference(LapText,
prevLap, false,false);


            if (prevLap == "00:00:00:000")
                bestLap = "";
            else
                bestLap = TimeDifference("00:" +
lapSplit, "00:" + prevSplit, true,false);


            lLapElement.text(bestLap);
            gLapElement.text(lapSplit);
            cLapElement.text(prependZero(currentLap,
3) + " / ");


            //$('#lapList').children('.lLap').css('c
olor', 'black');
            if (bestLap.indexOf("+") == 0)
lLapElement.css('color', 'red'); else
lLapElement.css('color', 'green');


            prevLap = LapText;
            prevSplit = lapSplit;


            if (Record(lapSplit)) {
                $('#bestLapTime').text("[" +
currentLap.toString() + "] " + lapSplit);
                highLap = currentLap;
```

```
                    // recalculate all splits to best
lap
                    RecalculateSplits(lapSplit);
            }

            rTime[currentLap - 1] = LapText;
            rLap[currentLap - 1] = lapSplit;
            rSplit[currentLap - 1] = bestLap;
            //playAudio('knockSound');

        }

        function RemoveLaps() {
            $('#lapList').empty();
            InitializeArrays();
        }
        // And it's better to keep the state of time
in variables
        // than parsing them from the html.
        var hours, minutes, seconds, milliseconds,
timer, timer2;

        function prependZero(time, length) {
            // Quick way to turn number to string is
to prepend it with a string
            // Also, a quick way to turn floats to
integers is to complement with 0
            time = '' + (time | 0);
            // And strings have length too. Prepend
0 until right.
            while (time.length < length) time = '0'
+ time;
            return time;
        }

        function setStopwatch(hours, minutes,
seconds, milliseconds) {
```

```
            // Using text(). html() will construct
HTML when it finds one, overhead.
            hoursElement.text(prependZero(hours,
2));
            minutesElement.text(prependZero(minutes,
2));
            secondsElement.text(prependZero(seconds,
2));
            millisecondsElement.text(prependZero(mil
liseconds, 3));
        }


        // Update time in stopwatch periodically -
every 25ms
        function runTimer() {
            // Using ES5 Date.now() to get current
timestamp
            var startTime = Date.now();
            var prevHours = hours;
            var prevMinutes = minutes;
            var prevSeconds = seconds;
            var prevMilliseconds = milliseconds;


            //timer2 = setInterval(function () {
            //    playAudio('secondTick');
            // }, s_beepFrequency*1000);


            timer = setInterval(function () {
                var timeElapsed = Date.now() -
startTime;


                hours = (timeElapsed / 3600000) +
prevHours;
                minutes = ((timeElapsed / 60000) +
prevMinutes) % 60;
                seconds = ((timeElapsed / 1000) +
prevSeconds) % 60;
```

```
            milliseconds = (timeElapsed +
prevMilliseconds) % 1000;

            setStopwatch(hours, minutes,
seconds, milliseconds);
        }, 25);
    }

    // Split out timer functions into functions.
    // Easier to read and write down
responsibilities
    function run() {
        running = true;
        $('#lChrono').text('RUNNING');
$('#lChrono').css('color', 'red');

        runTimer();
        toggleElement.text(pauseText);
        lapElement.removeClass('ui-disabled');
    }

    function pause() {
        running = false;
        clearTimeout(timer);
        //clearTimeout(timer2);
        lapElement.addClass('ui-disabled');
        toggleElement.text(resumeText);
    }

    function reset() {
        running = false;
        $('#lChrono').text('CHRONOMETER');
$('#lChrono').css('color', 'inherit');

        currentLap = 0;
        prevLap = "00:00:00:000";
        bestLap = "0";
```

```
            highLap = -1;
            lapSplit = prevLap;
            prevSplit = prevLap;
            topLap = 3600;
            topLapLine = "";
            lapElement.addClass('ui-disabled');
            RemoveLaps();
            pause();
            hours = minutes = seconds = milliseconds
= 0;
            setStopwatch(hours, minutes, seconds,
milliseconds);
            $('#bestLapTime').text(" - -");
            toggleElement.text(startText);
        }


    // And button handlers merely call out the
responsibilities
        toggleElement.on('click', function () {
            (running) ? pause() : run();
        });


        resetElement.on('click', function () {
            reset();
        });


        lapElement.on('click', function () {
            if (!running)
                return;

            if (currentLap >= MaxLaps)
                return;

            currentLap++;
            AddLap();
        });
```

```
$('#LapResults').on('click', function () {
    ShowArrays();
});


$('#oShare').on('click', function () {
    var msg = "";
    var dPlatform =
device.platform.toLowerCase();


    try {
        if (rTime[0] === "nop") {
            if (dPlatform === "android")
                alert("Nothing to Share");
            return;
        }

        msg = GetMessage();

        if (dPlatform === "android") {
            window.plugins.socialsharing.sha
re(msg);
        } else {
            //if
(device.platform.toLowerCase() === "win32rt")
window.plugins.socialsharing.share(msg,null,null,nu
ll); // Win 8.0
            //if
(device.platform.toLowerCase() === "windows")
window.plugins.socialsharing.share(msg,null,null,nu
ll); // Win 8.1
            window.plugins.socialsharing.sha
re(msg, null, null, null);
        }

    } catch (e) {
        // do nothing
    }
```

```
        });

        reset();
        if (running) run();
    });

});
```

That is a very long file but it does just what it does - controls a timer and it can pause it or restart it or even reset it, allowing for laps to be recorded. Examine the code at your leisure to determine how it does this. The most interesting part of the code is how it inserts laps into an existing list array dynamically so, every time you click "lap" a new row is added and computed for best lap or delta times with prior laps.

Countdown Timer Code File

The countdown timer is identical to the Timer only it counts downwards. The file is also reproduced below so you can see how it works:

```
$(function () {

    var cdElement = $('.scountdown').find('.ctime');
    var cdtoggleElement =
$('.controlButtons').find('.cdtoggle');
    var cdresetElement =
$('.controlButtons').find('.cdreset');
    var cdpauseText =
cdtoggleElement.data('cdpausetext');
    var cdresumeText =
cdtoggleElement.data('cdresumetext');
    var cdstartText = cdtoggleElement.text();
```

```
var counting = false;
var timer, timer2;


var InitialHours =
$("#cDownSliders").find('#hourSlider').val();
var InitialMins =
$("#cDownSliders").find('#minSlider').val();
var InitialSecs =
$("#cDownSliders").find('#secSlider').val();


var hours = InitialHours;
var mins = InitialMins;
var secs = InitialSecs;


function cdsetStopwatch(H, M, S) {
    cdElement.text(prependZero(H, 2) + ":" +
prependZero(M, 2) + ":" + prependZero(S, 2));
    }


$("#cDownSliders").on("slidestop",
"#hourSlider", function (e) {
    InitialHours =
$("#cDownSliders").find('#hourSlider').val();
    cdsetStopwatch(InitialHours, InitialMins,
InitialSecs);
    hours = InitialHours;
});


$("#cDownSliders").on("slidestop", "#minSlider",
function (e) {
    InitialMins =
$("#cDownSliders").find('#minSlider').val();
    cdsetStopwatch(InitialHours, InitialMins,
InitialSecs);
    mins = InitialMins;
});
```

```javascript
$("#cDownSliders").on("slidestop", "#secSlider",
function (e) {
        InitialSecs =
$("#cDownSliders").find('#secSlider').val();
        cdsetStopwatch(InitialHours, InitialMins,
InitialSecs);
        secs = InitialSecs;
    });


    function Decrement() {
        //timer2 = setInterval(function () {
        //    playAudio('secondTick');
        //}, s_beepFrequency * 1000);


        timer = setInterval(function () {
            secs--;
            if (secs < 0) {
                secs = 59;
                mins--;
                if (mins < 0) {
                    mins = 59;
                    hours--;
                    if (hours < 0) {
                        //playAudio('bellSound');
                        Vibrate(2000);
                        cdreset();
                    }
                }
            }
            cdsetStopwatch(hours, mins, secs);
        }, 1000);
    }


    function prependZero(time, length) {
        time = '' + (time | 0);
        while (time.length < length) time = '0' +
time;
        return time;
```

```
        }

    function count() {
        counting = true;
        $('#lDown').text('COUNTING');
$('#lDown').css('color', 'red');


        try {
            $("#cDownSliders").find("#hourSlider").s
lider('disable');
            $("#cDownSliders").find("#minSlider").sl
ider('disable');
            $("#cDownSliders").find("#secSlider").sl
ider('disable');
        } catch (e) {
            // ignore
        }
        cdtoggleElement.text(cdpauseText);
        Decrement();
    }

    function cdpause() {
        counting = false;
        clearTimeout(timer);
        //clearTimeout(timer2);
        cdtoggleElement.text(cdresumeText);
    }

    function cdreset() {
        counting = false;
        $('#lDown').text('COUNTDOWN');
$('#lDown').css('color', 'inherit');

        InitialHours =
$("#cDownSliders").find('#hourSlider').val();
        InitialMins =
$("#cDownSliders").find('#minSlider').val();
```

```
        InitialSecs =
$("#cDownSliders").find('#secSlider').val();
        try {
            $("#cDownSliders").find("#hourSlider").s
lider('enable');
            $("#cDownSliders").find("#minSlider").sl
ider('enable');
            $("#cDownSliders").find("#secSlider").sl
ider('enable');
        } catch (e) {
            // ignore
        }

        cdpause();

        hours = InitialHours;
        mins = InitialMins;
        secs = InitialSecs;

        cdsetStopwatch(hours, mins, secs);
        cdtoggleElement.text(cdstartText);

        // Loop if needed...

        if ($('#cLoop').is(':checked')) {
            count();
        }
    }

    cdtoggleElement.on('click', function () {
        (counting) ? cdpause() : count();
    });

    cdresetElement.on('click', function () {
        $('#cLoop').prop('checked',
false).checkboxradio('refresh');
```

```
        cdreset();
    });


    cdsetStopwatch(hours, mins, secs);
    cdreset();
    if (counting) count();
});
```

Data Analytics Code File

After you record some laps on the actual timer you can switch to the analytics page and see more detailed results and you may also share those results with others…

Appendix I: Atom - Electron Framework

Everything you have learned so far can be applied to Desktop Applications with simply minor changes. In Visual Studio, Windows already provides capabilities to build your Cordova application as a UWP app which runs in their stores and Windows Desktops. In Linux, you have the same option with the Electron Framework which also works in Windows if you want a simple tool for both environments. Why not do this? You can turn your mobile application into a native executable application for desktops in Windows and Linux and reuse all your code and technologies, including JQuery.

What is Electron

Electron is a web development framework developed by GitHub which produces native images (or executables) for desktops. Electron's main web site is **here** and you can download the framework from right there for Windows and for Linux.

Note that Visual Studio Code (VSCODE) itself is built using the electron Framework and it runs flawlessly on Windows, Linux and Mac. VSCODE is also open source so feel free to browse its source at GitHub but I tell you this, if VSCODE was written in Electron and it works so well, anything can really. It is worth trying particularly as a Cordova developer since there is so little effort involved.

ATOM vs VSCODE

There is a fantastic editor called ATOM that has been around for a while, also written with Electron and which is broadly adopted by many developers. **ATOM** is fantastic and very, very similar to VSCODE so feel free to use it.

I personally use VSCODE because I started out with it (or with Visual Studio) and it was already familiar and also because Microsoft seems to have put a lot of its weight behind it so it is heavily maintained, it has monthly releases, it has incredible extensions that are constantly  updated and it is also open source. The amount of people making useful extensions and add-ins for VSCODE is overwhelmingly good so it is difficult for me to look anywhere else.

ATOM however, without any argument, is just great so feel to try both and decide by yourself.

Porting Cordova to Electron

So, let's get quickly into what is needed to move a Cordova application into Electron. It is much simpler than you think and, while in keeping with my philosophy in this book, I will not be teaching you electron, I will be telling you how to turn cordova into Electron and that is 75% of what you need to know to start developing in Electron. The rest you can get from their great web site.

Why do this?
First of all - why do this?

- Because you can and it is easy;

- Why limit yourself? Why not reach a much larger audience than just mobile alone;

- Because LINUX: Linux honestly is in need of many more good apps and perhaps you can write a lot of them and provide them to Linux directly as an AppImage executable or as part of repositories and PPA's such as Ubuntu's LaunchPad. There is a store there and you can distribute your apps that way

You know, I have been using Linux for a long time and I love it. But I cannot help to think that many apps (not all, some are outstanding!) look faded or dated or way behind. This is not a criticism because I do love Linux and Open Source and I cannot believe how much has been achieved recently. But I think it is time to notch this up a bit and provide more than just the standard, kind of old looking faded apps (again, not all).

For instance, if you try to find a OneNote equivalent in Linux, good luck with what you get. I use some. They are great efforts but they are underwhelming. Why don't you write the next OneNote for Linux? You could with Electron, probably easily and you would have quite an impact because people are drooling for OneNote on Linux. Yes, you can use the Office 365 version but that is nowhere near as good as the client app.

So again, please do not take me as criticizing this wonderful platform. I just think we need to do a bit better with apps. If you look at an app like DIA (a wonderful substitute for Visio) or LibreOffice (another wonderful substitute for MS Office) they do great, they are great accomplishments, but they fall short in many, many areas.
With technologies like electron and cordova as well as others, you could write apps like these and blow our minds off and bring us into the 21st century. A number of apps already do this (GoDot, Android Studio, SmartGit, video players, music players, etc.) But many are in need of a revamp and modernization. Try to display a ribbon in LibreOffice and you will see what I mean.

Linux Images

You can produce packages with Electron in the form of RPM, Debian and other formats but I chose to use an executable format called an AppImage. I like AppImage because it is a distribution package that I provide once and it runs on most Linux distributions. If you provide a Debian package then you are talking about Ubuntu  and Mint and a couple of others. If you provide RPM, same thing... but AppImage runs in all of them as a standard without having to worry where you are. You can read more about AppImage here.

Let's Port Already

To convert a cordova application to electron you need to follow the next simple steps:

- Create a new folder for your electron project;

- Copy your WWW folder to this new folder;

- Get rid of the cordova references in your project's INDEX.HTML since we will not use cordova itself but rather Electron. So, remove the reference script to cordova.js; You may also delete INDEX.JS;

- On your header, add a line after the JQuery scripts to support JQuery like this:

  ```
  window.$ = window.jQuery =
  require('./scripts/Frameworks/jquery.min.js');
  ```

- Electron's main file is called MAIN.JS - this effectively replaces INDEX.JS. Here is an example MAIN.JS:

```javascript
const {app, BrowserWindow} =
require('electron')
const path = require('path')
const url = require('url')
const OS = require('os');

var CPU = OS.cpus()
var ARC = OS.arch();
var RAM = OS.totalmem();
var OSName = OS.type();;
var Platform = OS.platform();

// Keep a global reference of the window
object, if you don't, the window will
// be closed automatically when the
JavaScript object is garbage collected.
let win

function createWindow () {
 // Create the browser window.
 win = new BrowserWindow(
   {
     width: 480,
     height: 854,
     autoHideMenuBar: true,
     icon: path.join(__dirname,
'images/TideLock.png')
   })

 const ses =
win.webContents.session.clearCache(functi
on() {});
 win.setMenu(null);

 // and load the index.html of the app.
 win.loadURL(url.format({
```

```
    pathname: path.join(__dirname,
'index.html'),
    protocol: 'file:',
    slashes: true
  }))


  // Emitted when the window is closed.
  win.on('closed', () => {
    // Dereference the window object,
usually you would store windows
    // in an array if your app supports
multi windows, this is the time
    // when you should delete the
corresponding element.
    win = null
  })
}


// This method will be called when
Electron has finished
// initialization and is ready to create
browser windows.
// Some APIs can only be used after this
event occurs.
app.on('ready', createWindow)


// Quit when all windows are closed.
app.on('window-all-closed', () => {
  // On macOS it is common for
applications and their menu bar
  // to stay active until the user quits
explicitly with Cmd + Q
  if (process.platform !== 'darwin') {
    app.quit()
  }
})
```

```
app.on('activate', () => {
  // On macOS it's common to re-create a
window in the app when the
  // dock icon is clicked and there are no
other windows open.
  if (win === null) {
    createWindow()
  }
})
```

- Paste the code above into your MAIN.JS and save it. You are done... you can open this new folder in VSCODE and build it and debug it like you did with Cordova. A couple of more changes though before you do that since the app packages are different for electron - your JASON files need to change.

Your LAUNCH.JSON needs a configuration for running Electron. This will do - insert it into yours...

```
{
    "type": "node",
    "request": "launch",
    "name": "Electron Main",
    "runtimeExecutable":
"${workspaceRoot}/node_modules/.bin/electron",
    "windows": {
        "runtimeExecutable":
"${workspaceRoot}/node_modules/.bin/electron.c
md"
    },
    "program": "${workspaceRoot}/main.js",
    "protocol": "legacy"
},
```

You need a new PACKAGE.JSON to build and distribute your AppImage. Here is an example of such file (below). Please note that you use NPM to run and build this package so the instructions for installing Cordova are the same as for Electron. The only change is that you need to make sure Electron and Electron-Builder are installed (so make sure at some point you have issued a terminal command like this: **npm install electron -g**. And then also **npm install electron-builder -g**.

Here is the sample PACKAGE.JSON file for building and distributing an AppImage:

```json
{
  "_comment1"    : "To package app do NPM RUN PACK
",
  "_comment2"    :    "To    make    distribution
executable (appimage) NPM RUN DIST",
  "name"         : "nTimer",
  "appId"        : "com.madvox.nTimer",
  "productName"  : "nTimer",
  "description"  : "Some timers and counters",
  "author"       : {
    "name"       : "Madvox",
    "email"      : "admin@madvox.com",
    "url"        : "www.madvox.com"
  },
  "version"      : "1.0.0",
  "main"         : "main.js",
  "icon"         : "images/nTimer.png",
    "devDependencies": {
        "electron-builder": "~1.4.0",
        "electron-prebuilt": "~1.4.0"
    },
    "build"      : {
        "appId" : "com.madvox.nTimer",
        "dmg"   : {
        }
    },
  "scripts"      : {
    "pack"       : "build --dir",
```

```
      "dist"        : "build",
      "postinstall"  : "install-app-deps",
      "linux"        : {
        "target"     : ["AppImage","deb"]
      }
    }
  }
```

Appendix II: Open Source

I support Open Source. It has helped me a lot and I try to do what I can to help the effort. You can support Open source too by contributing source code, modifying existing code, distributing apps and binaries for people, joining teams on GitHub or LaunchPad, etc. But I urge you to consider supporting Open Source for the benefit of all of us developers and most users.

Ubuntu Store

If you did not know it, all Linux distributions have a package manager and in essence a store. I want to recommend that you make apps for Linux and put them at least in the Ubuntu Store since it is the most advanced one in my view. This store can be reached from **Ubuntu's LaunchPad**.

The LaunchPad is like the Google Developer Dashboard. You can create an account, join them for free and create your personally code repositories (PPA's) and keys and upload your software. People can then download it from their built-in stores. Remember that you do not have to give away your source if you do not want to and you can charge and ask for donations on your app. I personally do not do that but that is because I am not looking to make money from it but you could as it happens with Google, Apple and Microsoft Stores, even if it is outside of the LaunchPad.

Linux Development

I said it earlier - it took me a long time to take the leap into developing for Linux because I was usually put off, not by the awesomeness of its distributions but by the availability of applications and what they look or felt like.

I find some applications in Linux, and nowhere else, that only geniuses could have created but also that only geniuses can use and I think that is a serious problem that needs to be addressed. I use the GIMP a lot and I like it but I must admit, even though it provides pretty much everything you want, it's just hard to use and it looks dated compared to PaintShop Pro or Adobe Photoshop. A product that in my view is as good or better than those others should look a bit better and respond a bit better. Remember that this is not a criticism for I love these apps - it's an attempt to get them recognized as first class which is what they are - they just do not look it!

So, I also urge you to develop for Linux and help out in this space. Support Linux development - VSCODE gives you that opportunity right out of the box and so do Cordova, Electron, NodeJS and many other technologies.

Appendix III: Useful Resources

This is a tabulated collection of resources mentioned as hyperlinks above and also additional resources I think you may find useful:

Resources mentioned in this book

Resource	Type
Madvox Site	Madvox
Roguetoad Resources	Design
Madvox Videos	Design
nTime Video	Sample
Cordova Overview	Codova
Cordova Official Site	Codova
Cordova Latest	Codova
Cordova Plugins	Codova
Cordova Diagnostics	Codova
Cordova Merges	Codova
Manifest Guidelines	Codova
Responsive Design	Learning
Learning CSS	Learning
Learning HTML	Learning
Learning Javascript	Learning
Learning HTML and CSS	Learning
Learning Typescript	Learning
DOM Reference	Learning
Content Security Reference	Learning
Android Studio Bundle **- Windows**	Tools
Android Studio Bundle - Linux	Tools
Android Studio Documentation	Tools

Intel XDK	IDE/Editors
Xamarin	IDE/Editors
Microsoft Visual Studio	IDE/Editors
Visual Studio CODE	IDE/Editors
NetBeans IDE	IDE/Editors
IDEA IDE	IDE/Editors
Eclipse IDE	IDE/Editors
React-JS	Framework
Angular-JS	Framework
Ionic JS	Framework
JQuery Mobile	Framework
JQuery Plugins	Framework
Bootstrap	Framework
Sencha UI	Framework
HTML Kickstart	Framework
Kendo UI	Framework
Material Design UI	Framework
JQuery Demos	Framework
UX vs UI	Framework
Node JS Download	Tools
Node JS Documentation	Tools
GIT	Tools
SmartGIT	Tools
JAVA JDK	Tools
Electron Atom	Tools
Usability	Design
Google Design	Design
Google Best Practices	Design
AppImage	Design
Ubuntu LaunchPad	Catalog
AppImage Details	Design

Conclusion

I hope you found this technical book valuable. I enjoyed writing it in the hope that it will help someone get into and later progress to advanced development with Cordova and Electron. Admittedly, it was never a manual so I am not teaching you how to program the languages I am describing. However, you would agree that there are plenty of free resources to learn those at your leisure and many authors do a fantastic job in that space so I see no need to make yet another programming guide.

I hope that you can see how easy it is to port your web skills and in general your programming skills to Cordova and how easy it is then to move that to Electron which opens up additional access to the desktop (all desktops) thus maximizing your contributions and exposure.

Use twitter and even Facebook. I use Google Plus extensively. Network and connect with people that like what you do and contribute as much as you can or want to in the Open Source space if you wish. You are certainly needed there, we all are.

Glossary

Glossary of terms and abbreviations used in this book.

Term	Description
OEM	Original Equipment Manufacturer
IDE	Integrated Development Environment
SDK	Software Development Kit
UI	User Interface
UX	User Experience
JS	JavaScript
CSS	Cascading Style Sheet
HTML	Hypertext Markup Language
GPU	Graphics Processing Unit
IoT	Internet of Things
GML	Game Scripting Language
CSP	Content Security Policy
OS	Operating System
GIT	Version Control System
JDK	Java Development Kit
SPA	Single Page Architecture
MPA	Multi-Page Architecture
TS	Typescript
Transpile	Convert source code to source code
DPI	Dots per Inch
VCS	Version Control System
Stage	To add new or changed files
Commit	To save a snapshot of your code
Pull	To update local code from server
Push	To update server code from local
Manifest	Application Description and Permissions Log
Linux Mint	Possibly the best OS ever created
SRC	Square Root of Cucumber

Index

www.ingramcontent.com/pod-product-compliance
Lightning Source LLC
Chambersburg PA
CBHW071242050326
40690CB00011B/2234